DÉCOUPAGE
& DECORATIVE PAINT FINISHES

DÉCOUPAGE
& DECORATIVE PAINT FINISHES
Creating Treasures out of
Everyday Objects

RUBENA GRIGG

Reader's
Digest

THE READER'S DIGEST ASSOCIATION, INC.
Pleasantville, New York/Montreal

TULIPS, VIOLAS, AND ROSES decorate mostly secondhand-store buys

A READER'S DIGEST BOOK

Edited and produced by David & Charles Publishers
Photography by Di Lewis, *Book design by* Diana Knapp

The credits and acknowledgments that appear on page 141 are hereby made a part of
this copyright page.

First published in Great Britain in 1995

Library of Congress Cataloging in Publication Data
Grigg, Rubena.
    Découpage and decorative paint finishes / Rubena Grigg.
        p.   cm.
    Includes index.
    ISBN 0-89577-856-4
    1. Decoupage.   2. Finishes and finishing.   3. House furnishings.
    I. Title.
    TT870.G75   1996
    745.54'6—dc20   95-26077

Printed in Italy

CONTENTS

INTRODUCTION

My early childhood was spent in the depths of Lincolnshire, England, where I learned to appreciate a naturalistic way of life and the simple pleasures of the countryside. As an only child I spent many hours sketching, drawing, and painting, and, I am ashamed to admit, dressing up a very unwilling cat! Toy theaters fascinated me; papier-mâché and cutting collages, modeling with playdough and clay.

Only in the last 10 years have I begun to realize the lasting influence of those creative days and the importance of "play." Having reverted to a similar lifestyle, the ideas are flowing again, expressed now in the form of découpage. I do hope that something in this book will rekindle a similar flame for you, and give you many hours of creative pleasure.

Découpage is a fascinating art and delightful hobby. Meaning "cut out" (from the French *découper*), it involves carefully cutting out paper images and pasting them onto almost any surface, before applying varnish to give the impression of hand-painting or inlay.

Découpage is enjoying a tremendous revival. The beauty of it is that it calls for no artistic talent: as this book will show, after the simple basic techniques have been mastered all that is needed to create the most spectacular results is an eye for color and design, and a little patience.

It is very satisfying to transform shabby household items or thrift-shop finds into beautiful decorative pieces, and immensely pleasurable to be able to design and decorate a room in one's own choice of color and motif, incorporating fabric and texture into the scheme.

Throughout the book, paint finishes are used as background for the découpage. You may be inspired by a favorite piece of porcelain or a painting, by the flowers on a fabric, or the colors in a beautiful rug. Like me, you may draw your inspiration from the countryside; the possibilities are endless, and each design will be a reflection of your unique personality. I have included a wide variety of ideas, which should appeal to beginners and more advanced découpers alike.

There are over 70 projects and ideas, ranging from small decorative pieces to large items of furniture. Here you will find découpage projects for every room in the house: a coffee table for the living room, screens of varying size and description, Victorian and Edwardian toleware for the conservatory and a sumptuously romantic headboard decorated with cherubs and swags of roses. I have combined the use of paint and découpage on an elegant demi-lune table with sweet little floral cameos. Throughout the book you will find many projects using tin and toleware, which over the years has become a specialty of mine.

Découpage adds interest to many new items and can enhance old ones, particularly if they have become marked or stained. Subjects may be small or large; the larger the surface, the more scope there is for producing bold design work.

Chapter 1 provides all the information you will need to get started, with clear, illustrated step-by-step instructions showing you exactly how to prepare, decorate, and varnish your découpage project. We also show you how to achieve various background paint-finishes, and demonstrate techniques to transform otherwise ordinary pieces of furniture with hand-painted ribbons, leaves, bows, ropes, and tassels, and by applying craquelure and antique finishes. There is also a section devoted to problem solving with helpful hints and tips. A list of suppliers is found on pages 142–3.

There is no shortage of good-quality wrapping paper from which to create your own stunning designs, so choose your object, pick up the scissors, and start snipping!

HYDRANGEA brings this simple jug and bowl to life.

1

GETTING STARTED

 he materials for découpage are easy to find, and unlike many decorative arts, fairly cheap. Most items are available locally, but addresses of specialist suppliers are listed on pages 142–3.

◆　◆　◆　◆

◆ *materials* ◆

The following materials will enable you to complete most of the projects in the book. Any additional supplies required are listed in the individual project sections.

INITIAL PREPARATION
A supply of medium-grade sandpaper to sand your items before applying the undercoat, and very fine-grade sandpaper or other abrasive fine paper to rub down subsequent coats of paint and varnish for a smooth finish.

UNDERCOATING
A small can of acrylic primer undercoat, or red oxide metal primer for tinware, will suffice for most projects.

BACKGROUND COLOR
A small can of semigloss latex paint in a color of your choice.

BRUSHES
1 inch (2.5cm) paintbrushes of medium quality that will not shed many hairs are used for painting and varnishing. Keep a separate brush for varnishing. You will also need a No. 4 artist's brush for gilt decoration.

PAPER
Good-quality wrapping paper with plenty of definition, prints, or hand-colored photocopies. Paper must be printed on one side only, otherwise the pattern on the reverse will show through when you apply the varnish.

SCISSORS
Use a pair of small, pointed, and very sharp straight manicure scissors, which can be purchased from most pharmacies. You should not use a scalpel or craft knife because these will scuff the edges of the paper and make incisions which are too angular. They are also much slower to use.

GLUE
You will need ready-mixed, water-soluble, extra-strong

♦

wallpaper adhesive and a small glue brush.

CLEANING
Use a small sponge or a paper towel, dampened slightly with water, to clean off excess glue from your work.

GILDING
To paint antique gold decoration, you will need small tubes of gold and raw umber artists' acrylic paint. Use a No. 4 artist's brush to apply the gilt finish.

TACK CLOTH
A varnish-impregnated cloth for removing dust particles before each coat of varnish is applied. There are several good brands on the market.

VARNISH
Varnish has a tendency to develop a deep yellowish tinge as successive coats are applied, which will alter the colors of your work, so use the palest craft varnish you can find.

Throughout the book I have used a satin polyurethane varnish, which is available in many different sizes. Fast-drying, water-based acrylic varnishes are not suitable for découpage. They are fine when only four or five coats are used to protect a surface, but with the many applications required in découpage their appearance becomes milky. It is essential to use a good-quality pale

shellac (thinned) or polyurethane varnish, available in satin (flat, matte) and gloss forms. Gloss is the most hard-wearing, a flat finish the least, so for a durable flat finish, use gloss for all but the top two coats, which can be a flat finish. For makers and suppliers refer to pages 142–3.

BRUSH CLEANING
Use mineral spirits or a proprietary brush-cleaner to clean your brushes after using oil-based paint or varnish, and before washing them out in soap and water. If using alcohol-based products, such as shellac, clean up using denatured alcohol. Always read and follow the manufacturer's instructions.

ACCESSORIES
You will need a suitable *board* (or boards for larger projects) for pasting on the glue: pieces of Formica, white-faced hardboard, or the smooth side of ordinary hardboard (all available from building-supply stores) are suitable; a *craft knife* to lift pasted cutouts to adjust their position on the surface of your work; a piece of *white chalk* for drawing around the shape of the cutout design; screw-top *jars* or clean *containers* with lids (e.g. margarine tubs) make ideal receptacles for mineral spirits and water respectively.

(*NOTE* always store solvents in glass containers.)

SAFETY PRECAUTIONS

♦ Work in a well-ventilated area when using varnishes and solvents. Breathing fumes can lead to unconsciousness and permanent health damage. Wear a respiratory mask to protect against the inhalation of fumes.
♦ Take suitable fire precautions if working with flammable products.
♦ Always read the manufacturer's instructions.
♦ Wear thin, all-purpose rubber gloves when using denatured alcohol, mineral spirits, or turpentine, especially if you have sensitive skin or are prone to allergies. (These are available in multi-packs from most supermarkets.)
♦ Keep all materials out of reach of children. Use food containers with care: pretty colors in familiar containers are very tempting to a child.
♦ A cheap paper dust mask will protect against inhalation of dust and paint particles, particularly when using a power sander.
♦ Old paint contains lead: remember that poisons can be absorbed by skin contact, as well as by inhalation and swallowing.
♦ Most wallpaper pastes contain fungicides, which can cause skin irritation and dermatitis. Rinse fingers frequently and do not touch your face while working with adhesives.

♦

First Project –
A SET OF PLACE MATS

There is no substitute for "learning by doing," and this simple project will teach you the basics of preparation, application, and finishing, at the same time creating a beautiful addition to your dining-room table.
For a first attempt, these octagonal mats offer a lovely simple shape and a good even surface on which to work. The color I have chosen for the painted background is a gorgeous rich country green, which will show up flowers and fruit to their full advantage. It is important to use a darker background until you have become a little more experienced at cutting, and also to choose a paper with a similar background color.
A whole variety of designs look attractive. The design can be in the form of a garland, or overlaid to cover more of the surface. The flowers can be in small groups, or they can appear to "grow" from the base of the mat; alternatively, the paper cutouts can be arranged in a central posy. Whatever design you choose, try to make sure that it looks attractive from every viewpoint.
The molded edges are painted in a soft antique gold, which frames the design and gives a really professional finish. Once you have completed the first mat, you will be so thrilled with the results that you will be spurred on to make a set. Each one can be totally different in layout (so you will not become bored), but by using the same paper they will obviously be a set.

• materials list •

In addition to the items listed on pages 8–9, you will need:

A number of identically shaped particleboard or wooden place mats

Sufficient self-adhesive felt or baize to cover the underside of each mat

• preparation •

1   Paint the mats with acrylic primer undercoat and

allow to dry. Sand the edges and surface of the mats using medium-grade sandpaper. Remove dust with a tack cloth, then apply a second coat of acrylic primer and allow to dry. If the edges still feel rough, sand again. Overpaint with your chosen color, applying at least two coats until the finish looks perfect.

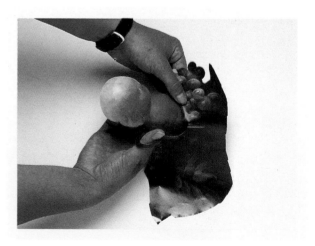

2   Cut out your motifs holding the scissors in a relaxed fashion. Always cut in the same direction for a natural flowing line around the edges. (Avoid square petals please!) If possible, turn the paper and not the scissors as you cut in and out of petals and leaves. Once you have mastered the technique you will never look back.

◆

OCTAGONAL PLACE MATS decorated with fruits and flowers cut from a horticultural calendar; the grapes and peaches were cut from wrapping paper.

Until you are used to cutting, it is a good idea to cut a little deeper into the pattern, rather than leave any background showing. Try to hold the scissors underneath the paper (see picture); it will be less likely to tear and will not reveal a white cut edge when stuck down on the place mat.

◆

To cut out a piece that is completely encircled by your motif, make a small incision with the point of the scissors and resume cutting from underneath as before. If this is impractical, cut through a stem or leaf, or around a petal, following the line where it will be less noticeable. The cut edges can be butted together so that the seam is invisible when it is stuck down. Complicated curling stems can be cut through in one or two places and carefully butted together to become a complete stem again when pasted onto the work.

When you have cut out a good pile of paper motifs, you can begin to make the design. Play around with the cutouts on the surface of your object, until the picture you create is well balanced in shape and color.

3 When you have placed the finalized design onto the mat, it is helpful to chalk carefully around the edge of the design, holding it in place with the palm of your hand as you do so, so that the shape is marked on the surface.

This gives a good indication of where to replace the cutouts when you have pasted them. The chalk marks can easily be removed with a damp sponge or paper towel later on. If you have decided to overlay the pieces of paper, when you have chalked around the edges, remove the uppermost cutouts to reveal the underneath shapes and chalk around those, too.

• creating a design •

For me, creating a design is the most exciting part. For our place mat project there are several options:

• MAKE A WREATH to encircle the place mat, slightly overlapping the flowers and leaves as they would in a real flower arrangement; this is known as overlaying.

• CREATE A POSY in the mat's center.
• PLACE MOTIFS in each angle.
• "GROW" THE FLOWERS from the base of the place mat. This design has the obvious drawback that it needs to be viewed the right way up to be appreciated fully.
• USE A MIXTURE OF STYLES. So long as they all originate from the same paper, they will make a delightful set and be the talking point of any meal.

• applying the glue •

1 You will need a pasting board(s), ready-mixed adhesive, glue brush, craft knife, small sponge, paper towels, and a container of water.

2 Select the first motif (if you are overlaying, take the underneath piece first); turn it face down on the board and brush on the glue from the center outward, spreading it evenly over the entire surface and making sure that the edges are covered. Lift, using your craft knife if necessary, and reposition within the chalk marks on the surface of the work.

3 Eliminate any air bubbles, blemishes, and excess glue with your fingers, dipping them in water if you find it helps (there is less likelihood of tearing the paper with wet fingers). Work from the center of the motif using a rolling movement of the fingers, and carefully wipe away excess glue with damp paper towels. If your fingers become sticky, rinse occasionally in water because they will remove the print from the surface of the paper. When the cutout is absolutely flat, press the edges down. Remember, glue may contain toxins and skin irritants.

4   When your decoration is finished, let it dry out.

5   You now need to remove any dried glue from the surface of the work. For this you will need a bowl of warm water and a small sponge (or paper towel). Dampen the sponge slightly and begin to clean the glue from the surface of the paper design, working gently from the center of the cutouts to the edges. Then clean off the background, taking care not to scuff the edges of the paper. If there are any loose edges, glue them down now and clean up carefully right away.

6   Tilt the work toward a light source to check that all the glue has been removed, and the work is clean and ready for varnishing.

♦ *gilding with antique gold* ♦

Fill the base of a glass jar or clean container with water, and squeeze a small amount of gold and raw umber artists' acrylic paint onto the lid. Mix together a portion of the colors with a little water, making it quite dark for the first application.

Brush the first coat of antique gold onto the rim of the work, always working in the same direction (going back will remove the gold particles). Approximately four coats is usually required to get a good depth; lighten each coat gradually by increasing the proportion of gold in the paint mix until the color is to your liking. Acrylic paint is water-based and will dry quickly, so you will be able to apply successive coats almost continuously.

Take great care to avoid getting paint on your fingers and transferring it to the surface of the work. Have some damp paper towels handy to wipe it off immediately, otherwise the gold particles will be illuminated by the varnish later on. The antique gold will "frame" your work, setting off the design and giving it a professional finish. Leave to dry before varnishing.

♦ *varnishing* ♦

1   Use a tack cloth to remove all traces of dust from the surface of the work. Wipe the edges first, then the surface, working in one direction.

2   After stirring the varnish, apply the first coat sparingly, so it does not become absorbed by the paper design and discolor it. Apply a thin coat, brushing it on around the edges first, then across the surface of the work, spreading the varnish evenly, and finally brushing it in one direction using the tip of the brush. Leave to dry for six to eight hours (or longer if recommended by the manufacturer – the time will also depend upon the air temperature in the room).

3   Subsequent coats of varnish may be applied more liberally, but the art is to spread it out quickly and evenly, remove any excess from the brush by wiping it on the side of a jar or can, and brush the varnish again in one direction, clearing the brush every so often and gently tickling the varnished surface with the tip of the brush. Repeat this until the air bubbles have been brushed out and the surface is as perfect as you can get it. *Remember to wipe the surface of the work with the tack cloth first to remove dust before applying the varnish.*

4   If the brush sheds hairs, or there are visible pieces of fluff in the wet varnish, remove them with your finger or work them to the side with the brush. Once they are removed, brush out the varnish in one direction again for a good finish.

5   Always leave varnish to dry thoroughly before using a tack cloth and applying another coat. The number of coats required will depend on the thickness of the paper used and the amount of overlaying in the design: the thicker the design, the more layers of varnish will be required to "lose" the edges. Approximately 10 coats should be sufficient for items of tinware, unless the design is overlaid a great deal.

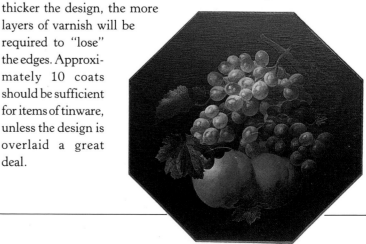

6 When at least 10 coats have been applied, and provided the edges of the paper are lost beneath the varnish giving it a wonderful depth and hiding any "stuck on" look (if not, continue varnishing), take a *fresh* sheet of the finest grade of sandpaper and gently rub the surface to remove any visible hairs and pieces of gritty dust that inevitably build up. Take care not to catch any painted edges. Do not be alarmed when the surface looks scratched; this will disappear with the next coat of varnish. Remember to use the tack cloth to remove the particles of dust from sanding before the next application of varnish.

Never attempt to sand your work until at least 10 coats of varnish have been applied. If you do, there is a strong possibility that you will rub through the surface of the paper, especially the edges. Tinware should not normally require sanding, unless the varnish runs. (See page 27 for some useful advice on solving découpage problems.)

The tack cloth is vital in obtaining a dust-free surface on which to work. If dust reappears on the surface at any stage, sand gently again to remove, and repeat the process. The final two coats must be absolutely perfect, otherwise the effect will be spoiled completely. Leave to dry for a day or two for the varnish to harden.

Objects that will take a lot of wear, such as trays, place mats, or coffee tables, should be given many more layers of varnish. Gloss is the most hard-wearing and can be used to build up the layers, changing to a satin for the final three or four coats. For place mats, trays, and decorative objects which may be placed on furniture, an adhesive-backed baize or felt can be cut to shape and applied to the underside of the work when all the varnishing is completely dry.

VARNISHING TIPS!

- Varnish yellows in direct sunlight, particularly on pale colors. I favor a clear polyurethane varnish in a satin finish, but you may like to use the hand-rubbed variety that has a more flat finish.
- Never immerse varnished objects in water because immersion may damage and discolor the varnish.
- Never shake a can of varnish because this will create innumerable air bubbles; always stir it instead.
- Some varnishes should be stirred to bring the cloudiness up from the bottom of the can.
- Keep some brushes specifically for varnishing.
- Never wear wool to varnish; an old cotton shirt is best.
- Always work in a well-ventilated area.
- Always follow the manufacturer's instructions.

SOME MORE BASICS

In addition to the skills you have learned while completing your place mat project, there are a number of other basic techniques with which you must be familiar in order to complete the projects in the remaining chapters. These are detailed below, followed by a few helpful hints which may help you out of a difficult situation.

Preparation of wood

◆ *complete stripping* ◆

Unless they are new, most wooden items will be covered with paint, varnish, or some other finish, which may require removal before you can begin work. If you wish to strip a piece of furniture completely, it may be better to use a professional furniture-stripping company who often collect and deliver at a reasonable price. This is well worthwhile for the amount of effort it saves on large items. However, there is no reason why most pieces can not be done by hand. A proprietary paint stripper, such as Zip-strip is the answer – follow the manufacturer's instructions and safety precautions, and wear thick rubber gloves. Remove handles, knobs, and fittings first, if possible. Any filling or repairs should also be carried out at this stage. Once stripped, treat the piece as for new wood, omitting the sanding sealer (below). If you own a power sander, your work will be cut by half.

◆ painted surfaces ◆

If you intend repainting the item, use medium-grade sandpaper to rub down the entire surface, working in the same direction as the grain in the wood. This will create a "key" or scored surface on which to repaint. Remove dust with a damp cloth and apply two coats of acrylic primer; allow to dry between coats. Always feel the surface by running your fingers over it. Sand down any rough patches with medium-grade sandpaper, paying particular attention to the edges and tops of drawers. Apply two or three thin coats of top color until a dense allover cover is achieved.

◆ stained wood ◆

Sand the surfaces with medium-grade sandpaper, working in the same direction as the grain in the wood. Stain "bleeds" into paint, and a barrier has to be created between the two. Coat the item with either a flat varnish (which may take up to six hours to dry), or with two coats of shellac thinned with a little denatured alcohol. Shellac varnish is fast drying, and it should be possible to apply the second coat in half an hour (keep your brush soft in a small amount of denatured alcohol in a *glass* jar). When the barrier varnish is dry, paint in the normal way with primer and topcoat.

◆ new wood ◆

Run your fingers over the surface to find any rough patches and rub down with medium-grade sandpaper, as before. Remove dust. If there are knots in the wood, apply sanding sealer, otherwise apply the first coat of acrylic primer undercoat and allow to dry. If the surface feels anything but smooth, sand the entire piece using fine-grade sandpaper and repeat the process. Apply two or three undercoats, letting it dry between coats. Apply sufficient coats of top color for a dense allover cover.

◆ medium density fiberboard ◆ or particleboard

Rub down the entire surface with medium-grade sandpaper, paying particular attention to moldings and edges. Remove dust and apply a coat of acrylic primer undercoat. Leave to dry, then run your fingers over the surface. If it has roughened anywhere, rub it down again using fine-grade sandpaper. Apply another two coats of primer undercoat, allowing it to dry between coats. Apply sufficient coats of top color for a dense allover cover.

Preparation of tinware

◆ materials list ◆

Red oxide metal primer
1 inch (2.5cm) paintbrush
Mineral spirits for cleaning up
Paper towels
Rubber gloves
Jar with lid for mineral spirits
Suitable wire brush (these are available
   in various shapes and sizes
   from hardware stores)
Car body spackle for filling holes

HIGH-NECKED EDWARDIAN jug, before preparation, with materials.

SOME OF THE ITEMS used in the projects, before preparation and decoration.

Many metal secondhand-store buys are perfect subjects for découpage, but they are often found covered in rust and chipped enamel. This situation must be rectified before you can set about beautifying them.

The term "tinware" covers a whole range of metal, including white, blue, and green enamel, tin, toleware, zinc, galvanized iron, and aluminum. With the exception of zinc and galvanized iron (dealt with separately on page 18), tinware is easy to prepare. Removing rust can be rather messy, but should you find something unusually rare, wonderfully shaped, or particularly pretty, which is covered in rust and you are keen to do it, there is no choice but to don a pair of rubber gloves and an apron, take your wire brush in hand, and get cracking!

1 Brush off all the loose rust from the surface, concentrating especially on seams in the metal, around the necks of jugs, joints where handles and spouts meet the main body, the edges of lids (which are often battered), spouts, and around hinges.

2 Give the tinware a good scrub. Clear the surfaces around the sink area and wash it thoroughly using a stiff brush or scouring pad and a cream cleanser. Dishwashing liquid on its own will not do the job of removing years of grime, grease, coal dust, paint splatters, bird droppings, discoloration from wine, and so forth. If possible, turn the piece upside down in a warm place to dry, but beware of dust if drying outside.

3 Once the tinware is completely dry, fill any holes or huge chips with a car body spackle (time-consuming, but essential if the vessel is to contain liquid – otherwise "dried flowers only").

Your piece is now as good as new in découpage terms, and the instructions hereafter apply to new and restored tinware alike.

4 Paint the piece with red oxide metal primer using an old, used, or cheap brush because there are tiny iron particles in the red oxide which are almost impossible to remove even with the most careful cleaning. It is a good idea to set aside a brush specifically for this purpose. Apply evenly, spreading it over the surface, because it does tend to run. Some people find this a difficult

medium to work with at first, but you will soon get the hang of it. I use it in preference to an ordinary metal primer because the density of cover is better and a second coat may be applied within an hour. Remember to stir well and follow the manufacturer's instructions. Allow to dry for approximately 30 minutes in a warm environment before applying the second coat. Leave overnight to dry out.

AFTER THE FIRST STAGES of preparation, the jug is cleaned and painted with red oxide metal primer. On the inside, this type of jug needs painting only down to the neck seam.

The red oxide primer retards rust to a certain extent and also gives a good "key" on which to paint, creating an even surface and filling in any dents in the metal. Even a brand new piece of enamel needs this "key," or else the paint will slip and slide, and it will take you twice as long to do.

When painting tall Victorian and Edwardian jugs which have narrow necks, the oxide needs to be taken down only as far as the neck seam on the inside, leaving the rest (which is unnoticeable) unpainted. Wide-necked jugs and items without lids should be painted on the inside, or else the final result will be rather ugly. It is advisable to leave the inner surfaces of breadboxes and so forth, unpainted if they are to be used for storing food, since ingesting red oxide paint is very unhealthy!

For the next stage there are two options open, depending upon the topcoat you have chosen.

5a If you are using a *pale color*, the next step is to undercoat with white acrylic primer, which is fast

drying, gives good cover, and is water based. Paint at least two coats, applying additional coats if necessary until the surface is perfectly covered. Now apply two or three coats of your chosen acrylic latex paint.

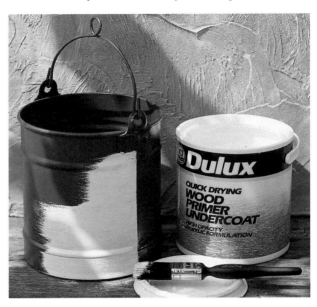

APPLYING THE FIRST COAT of acrylic primer to a red-oxided tinware bucket. Note that the inside is fully visible so it would look better covered completely with red oxide and two coats of paint, but this is optional.

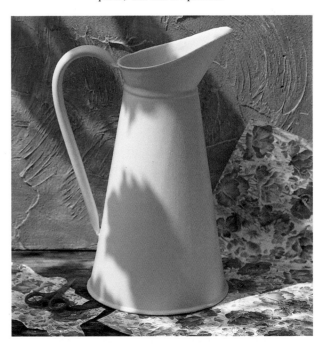

THE FULLY PREPARED JUG, with four coats of cream semigloss latex paint on top of the primer and red oxide. The jug is now ready for its découpage decoration.

5b   If you have decided on a *dark color*, there is no need to undercoat unless you wish to. Instead, apply three or four coats of latex paint until the surface is perfectly covered. Use either flat or semigloss latex paint. Occasionally a water-based paint refuses to adhere to a red-oxide primed surface, behaving as if the surface were greasy. A good tip is to add a little dishwashing liquid to the paint. **Never** use high-gloss enamel because it seems to be incompatible with the adhesive, and all your hard work in cutting an amazing design will be wasted when the paper dries and leaves the painted surface!

Flat latex paint is available in many sizes in a huge variety of colors; semigloss latex is also available in standard sizes and has the advantage of a slight sheen, making it possible to move the pasted paper motifs on the surface until they are in their correct position. It is therefore recommended for beginners. Clean brushes after use, according to the manufacturer's instructions.

◆ *zinc and galvanized iron* ◆

Zinc items are usually coated with a greasy flux which must be removed with degreasing fluid before priming. Degreasing fluid can be purchased from auto parts stores. Paint the liquid onto the object, covering the entire surface, and wash it off immediately. (If degreasing fluid is unavailable, an alternative is to soak the item in hot, soapy water.) Rinse well, leave to dry thoroughly, and it will be ready to paint with red oxide metal primer.

New galvanized iron tends to resist oxide and paint. The best preparatory treatment is to leave it outside to weather and lose its shine. However, I have painted new buckets with two coats of shellac before red-oxiding with successful results. There is a special primer available for galvanized metal, but it is lead based and therefore, in my opinion, should be avoided at all costs.

Paint finishes

Many items are made more attractive by the addition of an abstract, painted pattern applied to the background before découpage. Such additions are known as paint finishes. (See, for example, the photographs on pages 83, 104, and 106.)

With the exception of the decorative box on page 40, which has a fan finish, every paint finish in the book has been accomplished by using a natural sea sponge. It can be used open and loosely, so its shape and pattern become the design on the surface of the work – a broken paint-finish. Alternatively, it can be squeezed in the hand and dabbed closely to give a flowing movement on the surface, a technique which I call "close sponging."

The most delicate colors can be used together very successfully; a pale cream on white or white sponged on to deep cream, looks not only subtle but sophisticated. By using a dark color as a base and sponging on the same color, lightened several shades by adding white to it, is also very effective. Sponging on three complementary colors together (e.g. Venetian red, Payne's gray and raw umber, lightened with white in places) onto a base color of black will give a rich finish with great depth (see the mirror frame opposite). Experiment with color and techniques – you'll be amazed.

Sponging can be as sparse or as busy as you wish, but should never look regimented. Bright colors appear mellower under many layers of varnish or an antique finish.

A SECTION OF A MIRROR frame showing sponging using three complementary colors – Venetian red, Payne's gray, and raw umber – on a black background lightened in places with white and touched with gold.

Transparent paint glazes To produce lovely, soft, translucent colors, it is necessary to mix a glaze using equal parts of polyvinyl white glue (such as Elmer's) and latex paint, mixed with 1:4 parts water. This medium is low odor, fast drying, and keeps well in a screw-top jar or airtight container.

The various recipes for paint glazes throughout the book suggest using artist's acrylics. As an alternative I suggest using small cans of latex paint from the many mixed-to-order ranges of colors. Both mediums are excellent, but if you can find the required color in ready-mixed form, you may as well use it in the glaze – it is cheaper, and you will have some paint left over for future use.

◆ *sponging* ◆

◆ *materials list* ◆

Natural sponge
Paper towels
Clean container with lid
Polyvinyl white glue
Flat latex paint (colored), or white latex
    paint mixed with artists' acrylic colors
    of your choice
Old spoon for measuring
Water to mix

SPONGING SAMPLES: (top) yellow on white – the right-hand section also has white on top of the yellow; (middle) yellow painted background sponged white and when dry sponged yellow over the white; (bottom) pale green background close sponged with white and green together.

◆

Simple sponging Measure out equal parts of polyvinyl white glue and latex paint, mixed 1:4 with water. Combine the glue and paint mixture in a container to form a paint glaze. Sponge on as described on page 18. For two, three, and four color sponging, mix the glaze in a wide container and use the lid as a palette, adding acrylic tube colors, latex paint, or a mixture of both to achieve your desired color.

Parchment finish For the look of parchment, the background is cream *semigloss latex* with a few veins of soft ocher, raw sienna, and white. For a more intense color, I have used the following four colors for sponging: (1) yellow ocher (acrylic); (2) acid yellow (latex or acrylic); (3) minute amount of raw umber or Payne's gray (acrylic); (4) white (latex or acrylic).

Mix the paint glaze as before, using cream semigloss latex. Dip the sponge into the glaze first, and then into one or two of the colors and apply to the surface. Close sponge diagonally and create interesting patches of movement and color, building the pattern and density gradually. Clean the sponge thoroughly after use.

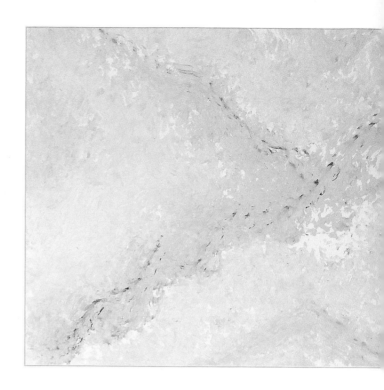

BUILDING UP A SPONGED *acid yellow finish, which will be toned down with white and cream.*

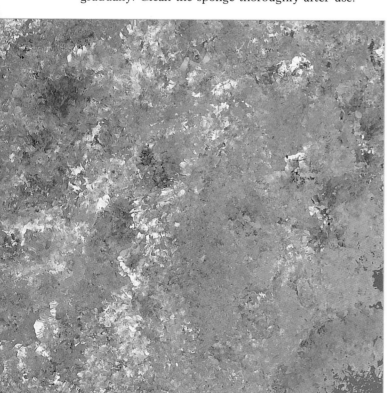

BUILDING UP SEVERAL *sponged colors to create the polished-slate effect for the coffee table on page 78.*

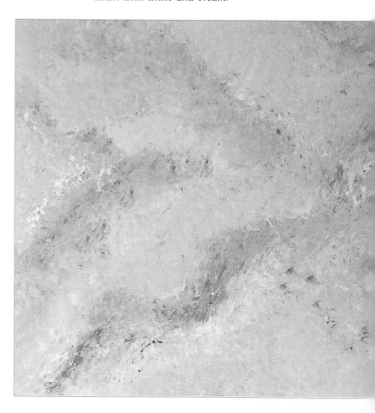

BUILDING UP A SPONGED *ocher parchment finish.*

◆

FAN FINISHES *As the sample board illustrates, it is possible to produce many different patterns using two or more complementary colors, or those of the same shade. These effects are painted with a No. 6 fan brush by dipping each side of the brush into a different color and by pulling the brush toward you along the surface, then returning to pull it through the colors. Experiment by wiggling and turning the brush to find your own techniques.*

◆

Hand-painted finishing touches

Hand-painted decoration can add a lovely finishing touch to your work. I think these look best in gold, as described below, but you can experiment with other colors if you wish. Practice on paper first. When decorating objects, keep a damp sponge or paper towel handy so any mistakes can be quickly erased.

• materials list •

Small tubes of artists' acrylics in gold and raw
    umber or two colors of the same family,
    one dark and one light
Artist's brush (No. 4 is an average size, but it
    will depend upon the piece of work)
Wide container with lid
Paper towels
Water for mixing
Blank paper for practicing

• twisted ribbon •

Squeeze small portions of gold and raw umber onto the lid and fill the base of the container with water. Mix a little of the colors together with the brush, wipe it on the edge of the lid, then dip it into the raw umber and, turning the brush over, dip the other side into the gold. Do not overload the brush. Make a brushstroke by pressing down on the paper, then releasing the pressure and twisting the point of the brush at the same time. Press–release–twist: these movements combined will give the twisted and shaded effect.

• for an uneven wired ribbon •

Sketch faintly first with chalk and paint in sections using the same method as for twisted ribbon, but returning to strengthen the shading.

• bows •

Use the same ribbon technique for the bow, which is tackled in separate sections (see diagram). The two shades of paint on the brush combined with "press–release–twist" are the basic steps to follow. It is a good idea to draw a bow onto the surface of the work in chalk, which can be removed when the bow is dry. It will take a little practice, but, like riding a bike, once you get the hang of it you will never forget.

• leaves •

Over the centuries leaves have been used to decorate furniture and are painted in many different forms. The following are simple ways to decorate and enhance your work. A No. 2 or 3 brush is best. Until you are confident, it may be helpful to draw a straight line faintly first in chalk. Using the two-color technique – dark color on one side of the brush and the paler (or white or gold) on the other – place the side tip of the brush on the surface with a little pressure, make a small stroke using the tip of the brush in a slight flicking movement which will form the point of the leaf, releasing all pressure as you do so. Draw a short straight stem-line with the tip of the brush and carry on into the leaf, add another leaf beneath it, and so on.

• curling stems •

Paint a thin curving line first. Add short stems and leaves on either side in the same way as before.

• berries •

Dip the tip of the brush into undiluted paint in the darkest color and stipple onto the surface using the end tip of the brush only; follow this by dipping the brush into white, again without water, and repeat.

COMBINE TWISTED RIBBON *with curling stems and berries to create a pretty border design.*

TWISTED RIBBONS

UNEVEN WIRED RIBBONS

BOWS

LEAVES

CURLING STEMS

BERRIES

◆

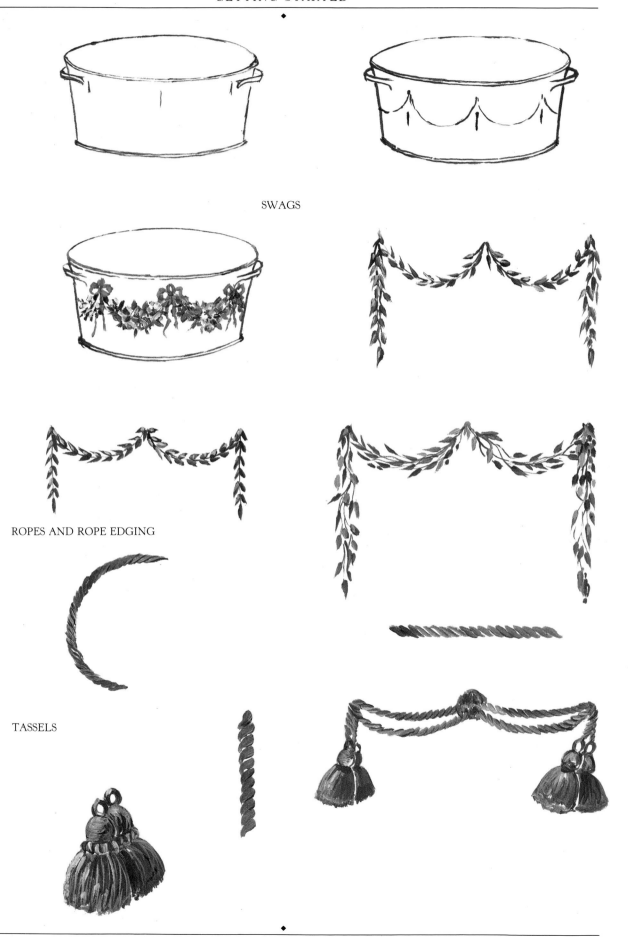

SWAGS

ROPES AND ROPE EDGING

TASSELS

• swags •

Swags, ribbons, and roses are my favorite theme. Quick and simple to paint, you will soon find they present no difficulty. Make three equidistant chalk marks and join them together with curved lines, shallow or deep, in the shape of a swag. Apply the découpage design, roughly following the curved lines. When the design is complete, dry, and cleaned up, the lines can be redrawn as a guide. Paint swags of bows and ribbons, leaves, or ropes. Leaves can be painted either from the center outward, or to meet in the middle.

• tassels •

Mark out in chalk first, then sketch the tassels in thinned-down paint to mark out their shape exactly. Fill in with the deepest color (raw umber in this case), shading the strands with gold until they look realistic. Highlight with white.

• ropes and rope edging •

The shape of the brush stroke is a shallow "S," laid down at an angle.

Aging and antiquing with craquelure

• materials list •

CRACKLE VARNISH

Two-bottle pack available from artists' supply-stores
1 inch (2.5cm) brush
Tube of raw umber artists' oil paint
Mineral spirits
Old tablespoon
Paper towels
Satin polyurethane varnish or shellac
Beeswax or white beeswax (for polishing furniture when it is completely finished and dry)
Soft cloth
Hair dryer and long extension cord

Almost all old furniture and some antiques which have been newly painted can be enhanced by a subtle craquelure finish. Reproduction furniture is often greatly improved by first painting and then adding an antiqued craquelure finish, but such pieces need to have the right "bone structure" to look convincing when finished.

Crackle varnish is sold as a pack, containing two bottles of varnish which interact to produce cracks. The first to be applied is a dark, slow-drying aging varnish, and the second is a very brittle, fast-drying water-based varnish. Because the water-based, brittle crackling varnish dries rapidly, it interacts with the slow-drying, flexible aging varnish and splits into hairline cracks. The process is unpredictable and the skill lies in knowing exactly when to apply the second varnish. The first

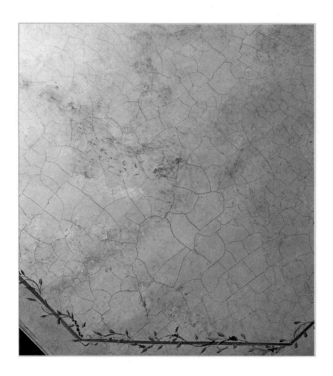

TABLETOP with an antique craquelure finish

should feel slightly tacky, "dry-tacky" and not sticky, before brushing on the crackling varnish.

• *applying a craquelure finish* •

1 If the piece is decorated with découpage, apply a single protective coat of satin varnish and leave to dry before applying the first craquelure varnish. If the piece is undecorated, the first craquelure varnish may be applied directly to the painted surface.

2 The first varnish should be applied thinly and evenly, brushing it out smoothly over the surface. When it is "dry-tacky" to the touch, brush on a more generous coat of the fast-drying water-based "crackle" varnish. Make sure the first varnish is covered entirely, otherwise you will be left with dirty-looking sticky patches! Leave to dry for approximately 60 minutes. If no cracks appear, a little encouragement is required by heating the surface with a hair dryer. The surface should be covered with delicate hairline cracks that are almost imperceptible. It should *not* look like clay which has cracked open in the sun!

3 The next stage is to apply the antique finish. Mix mineral spirits with raw umber artists' oil tube color – usually about 1 inch (2.5cm) of raw umber to about 2 or 3 tablespoons of mineral spirits. Mash the oil color with a little of the mineral spirits until smooth with no lumps,

then pour into the container adding more mineral spirits. (The consistency can be anywhere between milk and thick cream.)

4 Paint on; then, after 10 or 15 minutes, wipe off the decoration first with paper towels, leaving the antiquing fluid in logical places where dust would normally collect. Renew the paper towels frequently, "polishing" the surface and pushing the color into the cracks until the paper towels look almost clean. Leave the piece to dry overnight.

5 *The next day* apply a coat of a satin polyurethane varnish or shellac. Let it dry thoroughly. Paint with a second coat of varnish and leave to dry for a day or two. *NOTE* As the top coat of the craquelure finish is water based, the application of varnish is essential. For a satin-like patina, rub on a generous amount of natural beeswax polish, or white beeswax, and leave to dry for about 15 minutes. Take a soft cloth and buff up in the direction of the grain. The surface will look wonderful, and can be waxed several times and treated as any fine piece of furniture.

The above method of antiquing is probably the most common, but there are other antiquing compounds which can be applied to painted furniture, and so forth, which you might like to try:

• Scumble glaze may be used by mixing artists' oil paint and transparent oil glaze 1:8, adding the glaze slowly to the paint. (Light colors are not suitable for tinting an oil glaze because they will yellow in a matter of months.)
• Latex paint and/or artists' acrylics mixed with water to make a brown wash
• Brown wax polish
• White beeswax polish mixed with rottenstone and fuller's earth powder
(*NOTE* Do not apply varnish to this surface)
• Brown shoe polish
• Cold coffee

Colors used for antiquing are usually the earth colors raw umber, burnt umber, raw sienna, Payne's gray and terra verde.

• *paint categories* •

All paint is either water-based, oil-based, or alcohol-based. It is not possible to mix oil-based and water-based paints. Water-based paints, such as latex, will not easily adhere to a surface covered with an oil-based paint.

◆

Sometimes adding a few drops of dishwashing liquid may help, but it is more usual to create a barrier between the two by applying a coat of shellac which is alcohol-based.

Oil-based products include:
Oil primers, including aluminum and red oxide
Oil undercoats
Oil-based mid-sheen or satin paints
Gloss finishes
Scumble glaze (transparent oil glaze)
Enamels
Polyurethane varnishes
Craquelure first coat (the aging varnish – see page 25)
Wax polishes and liming wax.

Dilute products and clean brushes with mineral spirits; wash brushes in soap and water afterward.

Water-based products include:
Acrylic primer
Flat latex paint
Semigloss latex paint
Gloss latex paint
Latex paint glaze
Polyvinyl white glue (used in paint glaze)
Acrylic tube paints
Polyvinyl acrylic paints
Acrylic mediums and varnishes
Craquelure second coat (see page 25).

Dilute paint with water; clean brushes thoroughly in soap and water.

Alcohol-based products include:
Car spray paints
Cellulose-based enamels
Hammerite
Shellac
Cellulose lacquer
Wood stains.

The solvent for shellac and all the alcohol-based paints is denatured alcohol. Dilute shellac with a small amount of solvent before use, and keep a small amount in a glass jar (plastic containers will disintegrate) to stand your brush in to keep it soft – remember it evaporates.

SOLVING DÉCOUPAGE PROBLEMS

Here are some of the more common problems you may encounter – and their solutions.
◆ *TEARS* or surface damage to the paper cutouts when pasted. The paper, weakened by the wet paste, may occasionally tear when you are pressing out air bubbles and excess glue. It is usually impossible to butt the two pieces without the tear being obvious, so you must do one of the following:
(a) remove the cutout immediately with a craft knife and cut out another;
(b) if it is stuck down and drying, cut an identical piece and stick it over the damaged one;
(c) if the tear is small, overlay another cutout over the damaged part: slap a butterfly on it, for instance;
(d) as a last resort, soak off the cutout with water on a bristle art brush, working the brush behind it until it leaves the surface. Dry the piece off and start again.
◆ *TO MINIMIZE TEARS,* always let the decoration dry out before attempting to clean the surface up with a damp (not wet) sponge.
◆ *RUNS IN THE VARNISH,* especially where the varnish has collected around the base of a handle or under a rim, and run or dribbled and dried. With a sharp craft knife blade, carefully pare it off – don't dig the blade in deeply, otherwise you will go back to the base surface. Once removed, sand gently with very fine-grade sandpaper, remove dust with a tack cloth, and revarnish.
◆ *GOLD SPREADS OVER THE SURFACE* of the work with the first brushstroke when applying the varnish. There is nothing you can do to cure the problem, except to avoid it in the first place by using water-based acrylic gold underneath varnish. Apply a suitable finish, such as liquid gold leaf, enamel gold, gold cream or wax, after the varnishing stage.

◆

2
STYLISH ACCESSORIES FOR THE KITCHEN

*W*hether your kitchen is a warm hub of life and activity where the family congregate for meals, or a small, efficient, and labor-saving one, some items are found almost universally: a tray, breadbox, a set of canisters. Why not decorate something to brighten up your kitchen and provide an attractive focal point?

• • • •

ROUND BREADBOX

Add a little style to your kitchen! Smarten up a plain enamel breadbox by painting and designing it to match your color scheme, and it will certainly be a talking point among your family and friends. Darkest green or terra-cotta are particularly suitable background colors for a country home, but black or navy blue and dark rich red look more sophisticated in a town or city. You will enjoy using large flowers, which make a wonderful splash of color on any dark background.

• materials list •

ROUND BREADBOX

PREPARATION

Red oxide metal primer

An old 1 inch (2.5cm) brush

Mineral spirits

Paper towels

PAINTING

Small can of flat latex paint in a dark country
  green (or color of your choice)

1 inch (2.5cm) brush

DÉCOUPAGE

Good-quality wrapping paper of your choice

Small sharp scissors

Craft knife

Wallpaper adhesive

Glue brush

Pasting board

Small sponge or paper towels

Piece of white chalk

ANTIQUE GOLD

Small tubes of gold and raw umber artists'
  acrylics

No. 4 or 5 artist's brush

Lidded container or jar

Water to mix

VARNISHING

Tack cloth

Small can of pale satin varnish or shellac

1 inch (2.5 cm) brush

• preparation •

1   Prepare the breadbox as instructed on pages 15–18. If the breadbox is to be functional, do not paint the inner surfaces with red oxide primer.

◄ *LARGE FLOWERS brighten up an old breadbox.*

2   When the red oxide metal primer is completely dry, apply the dark green paint. (No undercoat is necessary as a dark topcoat is being used.) There is no need to wait for long between applications because water-based paint dries very quickly. Apply three or four coats until you achieve a perfect finish. Allow to dry completely.

• découpage •

1   Cut out a wide selection of flowers, leaves, and so forth. There are many possible designs, and with a little practice you will find out what pleases you best. Some of the cutouts could be formed into the beginnings of a design on a surface beside you, or you could glue on a couple of pieces and build up the design as you go along. It is sometimes easier to turn the box on its side in your lap and place several shapes on it to see if you like the effect. Chalk carefully around the edge of the motifs, leaving their outline on the box. This gives a good guide when you stand the box upright again, and begin pasting and attaching the pieces to the surface.

2   Turn each paper cutout face down onto the pasting board, and paste the glue evenly over the surface, making sure the edges are covered. Turn right side up using a craft knife and apply to the surface of the box, using the chalk marks for guidance. Work out the air bubbles and excess glue with a rolling finger movement, wiping the glue away with a paper towel. When the surface is flat, press the edges down. If desired, apply small motifs to the lid also. Leave to dry out.

3   Clean up the work with a small damp sponge, working from the center of the motifs out toward the edges to remove the glue from both the decoration and the background.

• finishing •

Apply an antique gold finish to the rim of the box, as described on page 13. Leave to dry, then varnish as described on pages 13–14.

◆

BLOSSOM BREADBOX *Here is another idea for decorating a breadbox – a simple white blossom design which is reproduced from a gorgeous Dutch masters painting published by National Gallery Publications Ltd. This paper requires careful cutting to remove the background, but fortunately it is black, too! Follow the step-by-step instructions on page 29, changing the color of the paint to suit.*

DECORATED WITH *an easy-to-cut motif, these canisters will cheer up any kitchen.*

A COLLECTION OF CANISTERS

Canisters are plentiful in secondhand stores and at flea markets; perhaps you have a set at home. They come in various shapes and sizes, but do check that the lids belong to the bases because they are frequently an exact marriage and ill-fitting. The set of canisters in the photograph is painted in a dark country green and decorated in a bright, cheerful primula design, which is very simple to cut and quick to do.

◆ materials list ◆

CANISTERS OF VARIOUS SIZES

PREPARATION
Red oxide metal primer
An old 1 inch (2.5cm) brush
Mineral spirits
Paper towels

PAINTING
Small can of flat latex paint in dark
   green
1 inch (2.5cm) brush

DÉCOUPAGE
Wrapping paper
Small sharp scissors
Craft knife
Wallpaper adhesive
Glue brush
Pasting board
Small sponge or paper towels

ANTIQUE GOLD
Small tubes of gold and raw umber artists'
   acrylics
No. 4 artist's brush
Lidded container or jar
Water to mix

VARNISHING
Tack cloth
Small can of satin polyurethane varnish or
   shellac
1 inch (2.5cm) brush

◆ preparation ◆

1   Prepare the tinware as described on pages 15–18. If the canisters are to be used for storing food, do not paint the inner surfaces with red oxide primer.
2   When the red oxide is dry, apply two coats of dark green latex paint to the outer surface of each canister, letting it dry after each coat. Turn the canisters upside down and paint the bases.

◆ découpage ◆

1   Cut out blocks of flowers and leaves, and apply in a random fashion around the base of each canister. Fill in with single flowers and leaves wherever necessary.
2   Turn each cutout face down onto the pasting board and apply the glue evenly, making sure the edges are covered. Turn right side up using a craft knife, and apply to the surface, working out any air bubbles and excess glue with your fingers and wiping off with a paper towel. When the surface is flat, press down the edges. Leave to dry.
3   Decorate the lids and leave them to dry.
4   Clean up the work and background paint with a damp sponge, working from the center of the design out toward the edges. Leave to dry.

◆ finishing ◆

Apply an antique gold finish to the canister rims, as described on page 13. Leave to dry, then varnish as described on pages 13–14.

FAT COFFEEPOT

*The squat, sturdy shape of this old coffeepot
attracted me to buy it. The lovely paper includes
antique roses and lilies in its design, and is one
that I have used several times in the book. I think
it is ideal for the coffeepot.*

• materials list •

COFFEEPOT
PREPARATION
Red oxide metal primer
An old 1 inch (2.5cm) brush
Mineral spirits
Paper towels
PAINTING
Small can of white acrylic primer
Small can of semigloss latex paint in cream
1 inch (2.5cm) brush
DÉCOUPAGE
Wrapping paper with large blooms
Small sharp scissors
Craft knife
Wallpaper adhesive
Glue brush
Pasting board
Small sponge or paper towels
ANTIQUE GOLD
Small tubes of gold and raw umber artists'
    acrylics
No. 4 artist's brush
Lidded container or jar
Water to mix
VARNISHING
Tack cloth
Small can of satin polyurethane varnish or
    shellac
1 inch (2.5cm) brush

• preparation •

1 Prepare the pot as described on pages 15–18. If the
pot is to be functional, do not apply red oxide primer to
the inner surface.
2 When the red oxide is completely dry, apply at least
two coats of white acrylic primer until the surface is well
covered, allowing to dry between coats. Turn the pot
upside down and paint the base.
3 Paint the pot with semigloss latex – two or three coats
will probably be required – and let it dry.

• découpage •

1 Select a few beautiful blooms and cut them out
meticulously: any mistakes will be very noticeable on the
pale background. Choose a few flowers with long curling

stems to glue at the base of the handle to bring the designs on the two sides together. A fairly delicate and curving bloom or bud with a twisting stem would enhance the decoration on the lid.

2   Turn each cutout face down onto the pasting board and spread the glue evenly over the surface, making sure the edges are covered. Turn right side up using a craft knife, and stick onto the pot, working out air bubbles and excess glue with your fingertips. Leave to dry.

3   Using a small damp sponge, and working from the center of the design out toward the edges, clean the excess glue from both the decoration and the background.

◆ *finishing* ◆

Apply an antique gold finish to the rim and handle of the coffeepot, as described on page 13. Leave to dry, then varnish as described on pages 13–14.

◆

3
TRANSFORMING
EVERYDAY ITEMS

*M*ost of us have things we use almost without noticing how shabby they have become; a tea-caddy, cookie jar, or tin box perhaps, an old tray, boxes in numerous shapes and sizes tucked away in a cupboard or at the back of a drawer. Let them see the light of day, give them a coat of paint, cut a pretty design, and they will become both useful and decorative. In this chapter there are several such items; you may have other things at home which would benefit from a facelift, and I hope the following ideas will inspire you.

◆ ◆ ◆ ◆

RED TIN BOX WITH ROSES

An unusually shaped tin box, which once held cookies or chocolates, a rusty black deedbox, or any old tin box in fact, all can be given a new lease on life becoming, after a complete facelift, much admired objects of beauty.

• materials list •

AN OLD TIN BOX

PREPARATION

Red oxide metal primer

An old 1 inch (2.5cm) brush

Mineral spirits • Paper towels

PAINTING

Small can of dark red flat or semigloss latex
  paint

1 inch (2.5cm) brush

DÉCOUPAGE

8 lovely full blown roses, leaves, and stems, cut
  from 3 sheets of wrapping paper

Small sharp scissors • Craft knife

Wallpaper adhesive • Glue brush

Pasting board

Small sponge or paper towels

Piece of white chalk

ANTIQUE GOLD

Small tubes of gold and raw umber artists'
  acrylics

No. 4 artist's brush

Lidded container or jar • Water to mix

VARNISHING

Tack cloth • Small can of satin polyurethane
  varnish

1 inch (2.5cm) brush

FINAL TOUCHES

Suitably sized piece of self-adhesive felt

Kitchen scissors

• preparation •

1   Prepare the box as described on pages 15–18.
2   When the red oxide metal primer is completely dry, apply at least four coats of the dark red paint. This may look pale red or even pink on the box, but the color will intensify and darken as more coats are applied. Allow each coat to dry before applying the next.

◄ A RUSTY DEEDBOX is given a new lease on life.

• découpage •

1   Cut out approximately 8 roses with stems and leaves. Take care to cut around the thorns – well worth the effort because they look marvelous against the background.
2   Arrange the flowers and leaves in a circular or oval shape, overlapping slightly. When you are happy with the design, hold it down with the palm of your hand and, with a piece of white chalk, draw around the design to leave an outline. This will be a useful guide when you are pasting and trying to remember where each piece was placed in your original design.
3   Turn each paper cutout face down onto the pasting board. Apply the glue evenly over the surface, making sure the edges are covered and pasting over the fine stems on the board. A craft knife will be helpful for lifting them.
4   Turn the cutouts right side up using a craft knife and line up with the chalk marks on the box, gently straightening out each flower and stem until it is flat (thin stems can easily crease). Work out the air bubbles and excess glue with a rolling finger movement, wiping away glue with a paper towel and pressing down the edges when the cutout is flat. When complete, leave to dry.
5   Clean up the surface of the design and background carefully with damp paper towels or a small sponge. Leave to dry.

• finishing •

Apply an antique gold finish to the rim of the box, as described on page 13. Leave to dry, then varnish as described on pages 13–14. Apply the first coat of varnish sparingly to avoid the wonderful white roses absorbing the varnish and becoming discolored. Leave to dry for a day or two.

• final touches •

Place the base of the box onto the paper backing of the self-adhesive felt, and draw around it to mark out the shape. Cut along the marked lines, peel off the backing, and stick the felt to the base of the box to protect your furniture and provide a professional finish.

FLOWERED TRAY

This old tray had been kicking around the house for years. Its composition is unknown, but that doesn't matter; it was paintable and ripe for transformation. This project uses a simple sponged-on paint-finish to create an interesting background.

• materials list •

ANY NONMETALLIC TRAY

PREPARATION

Fine-grade sandpaper

PAINTING

Small can of white acrylic primer

Small can of white semigloss latex paint

1 inch (2.5cm) brush

Polyvinyl white glue

Small can of cream flat or semigloss
    latex paint

Small natural sponge

Container for mixing glaze

Water to mix

DÉCOUPAGE

Wrapping paper with flower heads

Small sharp scissors

Craft knife

Wallpaper adhesive

Small glue brush

Pasting board

Small sponge or paper towels

ANTIQUE GOLD

Small tubes of gold and raw umber artists'
    acrylics

No. 4 artist's brush

Lidded container or jar

Water to mix

VARNISHING

Tack cloth

Small can of pale satin polyurethane varnish or
    shellac

1 inch (2.5cm) brush

Fine-grade sandpaper

• preparation •

1 Apply two or three coats of acrylic primer, allowing it to dry between coats. (Acrylic paint is fast drying because it is water based.)

2 Paint with two coats of white semigloss latex paint.

3 Mix a paint glaze by combining one tablespoon of white glue with one tablespoon of cream flat or semigloss latex paint and two or three tablespoons of water.

4 Dip the tip of the damp sponge into the glaze and squeeze out. With a light movement, dab the sponge over the surface of the tray, moving the sponge in different directions to avoid a regimented design. This should take no more than 30 minutes to dry.

• découpage •

1 Cut a good number of flower heads and a few leaves. Lay on the edge of the tray in a line or in small groups.

2 Set out pasting board, wallpaper paste, glue brush, small sponge, and a container of water. Paste each flower head separately and apply to the tray. A craft knife will be helpful to lift small pasted cutouts from the board. Continue until the design around the edge is finished.

3 A second line of flower heads may be applied. My tray originally appeared rather bare, but when another line of flower heads was added in a scalloped shape, the tray took on a much more cheerful appearance. A small posy of flowers decorates the center of the tray.

4 When the pasted-on design is dry, clean off the excess glue from the flowers and the background with a damp sponge, working outward from the center of the blooms and taking care not to scuff the edges. Allow to dry.

• finishing •

Apply an antique gold finish around the tray, as described on page 13. Allow to dry, then varnish as described on pages 13–14. If the tray is to be functional, it will require at least 10 coats of varnish, but you could get away with fewer if it is for decorative purposes only.

EASY TO CUT and glue, pansies over a simple sponged paint-finish beautify an old tray. The object to the top right of the tray, similarly decorated, is an Edwardian bedpan.

EDWARDIAN ENAMEL JUG

This beautiful old Edwardian jug was found quite fortuitously. It was discolored, dirty, and green with algae when it was spotted in a friend's greenhouse where it had been used for watering the plants. Needless to say, it was rescued immediately – with stunning results.
The jug was painted in a gardenia color, and simply splotched all over very lightly with a sponge dipped in a soft ocher paint glaze. This is a speedy way of achieving a broken paint-finish.

THESE EXQUISITE LILIES
and deep blue morning glories blend beautifully with the sponged background to create a delicate, yet rather sophisticated effect, which would fit into almost any setting.
Photographed on an antique embroidered silk shawl against a little hand-painted Victorian mirror and filled with sweet-smelling stargazer lilies, it is accompanied by one of my favorite birthday gifts, a heavily gilded Minton compote holding fragile white roses gathered from a friend's garden to complete the light theme. The wrapping paper is by Caspari.

◆

◆ *materials list* ◆

ENAMEL JUG

PREPARATION
Red oxide metal primer
An old 1 inch (2.5cm) brush
Mineral spirits
Paper towels

PAINTING
Small can of white acrylic primer
Small can of cream semigloss latex paint
1 inch (2.5cm) brush
Polyvinyl white glue
Small can of white acrylic flat or eggshell paint
Small amount of yellow ocher artists' acrylic
    tube paint
Small natural sponge
Lidded container or jar
Water to mix

DÉCOUPAGE
Wrapping paper
Small sharp scissors
Craft knife
Wallpaper adhesive
Glue brush
Pasting board
Small sponge or paper towels

ANTIQUE GOLD
Small tubes of gold and raw umber artists'
    acrylics
No. 4 artist's brush
Lidded container or jar
Water to mix

VARNISHING
Tack cloth
Small can of satin polyurethane varnish
1 inch (2.5cm) brush

◆ *preparation* ◆

1 Prepare the jug as described on pages 15–18.
2 When the red oxide metal primer is dry, apply two or three coats of white acrylic primer, allowing it to dry between coats.
3 Apply two or three coats of cream semigloss latex until the surface looks perfect. Allow to dry between coats.
4 Prepare a paint glaze by combining one tablespoon of white glue, one tablespoon of white acrylic flat or eggshell paint, a small squeeze of yellow ocher artists' acrylic, and three tablespoons water to mix. Squeeze the sponge out in clean water and dab onto paper towels to remove excess moisture. Dip part of the sponge into the ocher glaze, and lightly sponge over the surface of the jug using a random motion. Leave to dry.

◆ *découpage* ◆

1 Cut out the lilies and morning glories, taking care with the fine curling stems. If you find them difficult to handle, cut them into sections and butt them together when they are pasted onto the surface.
2 Place each cutout face down onto the pasting board and brush on the glue evenly over the surface, making sure the edges are covered. Turn right side up – the craft knife will be useful for this and for lifting the curling stems into position – and place on the surface of the jug.
NOTE It is tricky to glue on large paper cutouts absolutely flat because the surface is bulbous and they tend to crease. When cutouts are wet with paste they do stretch slightly, so take care when you are pressing out the glue, or make a small incision on the outer edge of a flower to avoid creasing. Leave to dry.
3 Clean off the excess glue from the work using a small damp sponge or paper towels.

◆ *finishing* ◆

Apply an antique gold finish to the rim of the jug, as described on page 13. Leave to dry, then varnish as described on pages 13–14, taking care that the varnish does not run from the handle or the top rim.

◆

◆

DECORATIVE BOX

Most of us have one or two old boxes tucked away in a cupboard or relegated to the back of a drawer. The box in the picture was a fifties jewelry box, which had been covered in thin leather and lined in silk. The leather took time to soak off, but afterward the pine box rubbed down easily. The paint effect was done with a fan brush, and the cords and tassels hand-painted. Odd pieces of fabric have been used to line the box so it can revert to its original function, or double up as a small sewing box.

ROPES AND TASSELS *on a fan finish adorn this beautiful box.*

◆

• materials list •

WOODEN BOX WITH HINGED LID

PREPARATION
Medium-grade and fine-grade sandpaper

PAINTING
Small can of white acrylic primer
1 inch (2.5cm) brush, or smaller
Small can of terra-cotta flat latex paint, or
    another color of your choice
Small can of white flat latex paint, or a small
    tube of Chinese white artists' acrylic tube
    paint • No. 6 fan brush
Lidded container

CAMEO
Piece of white chalk
Small can of cream flat or semigloss latex paint
Small brush to apply – a cheap, soft glue brush
    would fit the bill

DÉCOUPAGE
Good-quality wrapping paper, or a picture taken
    from a gardening or horticultural calendar, or
    a botanical print
Small sharp scissors • Craft knife
Wallpaper adhesive
Glue brush • Pasting board
Small sponge or paper towels

HAND-PAINTED DECORATION
Small tubes of gold and raw umber artists' acrylics
White paint, as listed above
No. 4 artist's brush
Lidded container • Water to mix

VARNISHING
Tack cloth
Small can of satin polyurethane varnish or
    shellac
1 inch (2.5cm) brush • Mineral spirits

FINAL TOUCHES
Suitably sized piece of self-adhesive baize or felt,
    and fabric or wallpaper to line interior

• preparation •

1   Repair (if necessary) and sand your box.
2   Remove dust and dirt from the inside and out, then apply a coat of white acrylic primer. Let it dry before applying the second and third coats.
3   Apply two coats of terra-cotta flat latex paint (or color of your choice), and let it dry. Take the fan brush and dip one side of it into white paint, the other into the terra-cotta. Pull it toward you, wiggling it in any direction, replenishing either or both colors as you work (see page 21). Cover the entire surface with the pattern, propping up the lid to avoid it from sticking closed. Leave the box to dry.

• the cameo •

Draw the oval shape of the cameo on top of the paint-finish with white chalk (it can be dusted off to make alterations). With a small brush, apply two or three coats of white primer, letting it dry between coats. When the cameo looks solid white, apply the cream-colored paint – two coats should be sufficient.

• découpage •

1   Choose a few beautiful cutout blooms and arrange within the cameo.
2   When the design looks balanced, glue on the underneath pieces first. Turn each paper cutout face down on the pasting board and brush the glue evenly over the surface, making sure the edges are covered. Place the cutout into position, press air bubbles and excess glue out to the edges, and wipe with a paper towel. When the flowers are flat, press the edges down. Leave to dry.
3   Using a small piece of damp sponge or a paper towel, remove excess glue from the background paint and from the design. Leave to dry.

• ropes and tassels decoration •

1   Using a No. 4 artist's brush, mix a small portion of raw umber and gold together, blending it rather dark to start. Paint a rope around the cameo (see page 25) and let it dry. Go over it a second time, highlighting logical areas.
2   Make small chalk marks to indicate the center of the front, back, and sides, and continue with the rope design. Don't worry if your line isn't absolutely true, it can become a double cord to balance things out, as here.
3   Finally, draw the tassels (see page 25) with a pale mix of white and raw umber; fill in with deeper umber and gold until the tassels look realistic and highlight with white. Decorate the box's keyhole if there is one.

• finishing •

When the work is dry, remove dust and apply a coat of varnish to the oval cameo. Subsequent coats should cover the entire box. Prop the lid open to avoid sticking. Cover the base of the box with self-adhesive baize or felt, and line with fabric or wallpaper.

CHRISTMAS PLATTERS AND PLATES

Unusually shaped platters or sizeable plates are devilishly difficult to find, unless they are of porcelain or pottery. Purely functional new enamelware is available from department stores, and you might be able to find a selection of unusual items in white enamel which could be decorated; failing that, use old crockery plates. During the Christmas season there never seems to be enough plates in the house to use for candies and nuts and these will be a welcome addition. Remind willing helpers after the party that they must not be immersed in water.

◆ materials list ◆

PREPARATION – ENAMEL PLATTERS AND PLATES
Small can of red oxide metal primer
An old 1 inch (2.5cm) brush
Mineral spirits ◆ Paper towels

PREPARATION – POTTERY PLATES
A paint glaze mixing 1 tablespoon of polyvinyl
   white glue with one of white latex paint to 2
   parts water. Apply two coats and allow to dry
   thoroughly before painting on a color.
1 inch (2.5cm) brush, or smaller

PAINTING
Small can of flat latex paint in a dark green or
   red

DÉCOUPAGE
Hand-painted Christmas giftwrap, illustrated with
   holly, ivy, mistletoe, or other Christmastime
   flora
Small sharp scissors
Craft knife
Wallpaper adhesive
Glue brush
Pasting board
Small sponge or paper towels

ANTIQUE GOLD
Small tubes of gold and raw umber artists'
   acrylics
No. 4 artist's brush
Lidded container or jar
Water to mix

VARNISHING
Tack cloth
Small can of satin polyurethane varnish or
   shellac
1 inch (2.5cm) brush ◆ Mineral spirits

◆ preparation ◆

1   Prepare enamel plate(s) as described on pages 15–18.
2   When the oxide or paint glaze is dry, apply two or three coats of your chosen color, brushing the paint on in one direction for a neat finish and allowing it to dry between coats.

◆ découpage ◆

1   Carefully cut one or two attractive sprays or blooms and leaves for each plate.
2   Turn each cutout face down onto the pasting board and brush the glue evenly over the surface, making sure that the edges are covered. Using a craft knife, turn right side up and position on the plate, working out any excess glue and air bubbles with a rolling movement of the fingers. When the cutout is flat, press down the edges and wipe away the glue with damp paper towels.
3   When the design is finished, leave it to dry completely before cleaning up the surface with a damp sponge or a paper towel to remove any dried glue.

◆ finishing ◆

Apply an antique gold finish to the outer edge of the plate, as described on page 13, or decorate it with leaves (see page 22). Leave to dry, then varnish as described on pages 13–14.

▶ CHRISTMAS PLATTERS *have been decorated with hand-painted paper by Sandra Wall-Armitage. It was tricky to dissect the mistletoe and holly from the ivy, but well worth the effort.*

4
SPRINGTIME

*I*n England, snowdrops, hellebores and crocuses provide early color in the garden; now with the first warm days and birdsong in the air, wild primroses cover the high banks along the lanes, and deep purple violets and buttercups are showing their tiny faces.

A most inspiring paper, which has been skillfully handpainted by Sandra Wall-Armitage, depicts violets, which are so realistic one can almost feel their fragility and smell their delicate fragrance, a variegated ivy, crocuses, buttercups, and snowdrops – the first breath of spring!

One sheet goes a long way because it is possible to dissect each species separately. The crocuses on the paper appear lifelike, but this quality tends to be diminished when they are cut out unless treated with imagination. Because they are so straight, they can be tucked under one another in the design to give movement and life.

◆ ◆ ◆ ◆

BOTTLE COASTERS

Primrose-yellow and leaf-green paint are a perfect foil for the spring flowers on the design. Simple paint-finished backgrounds add more interest if you feel like experimenting. A pair of pretty coasters would be a unique and individual gift, and a most acceptable wedding present for a spring bride and groom, especially if they were accompanied by two bottles of fine champagne!

▶ *TINY GALLERIED TRAYS The coasters and trays use different flowers cut from the same paper. The two trays have been decorated with spring flowers applied to a primrose-yellow background in exactly the same way as the coasters. The violets require accurate cutting and careful pasting. The stems of the crocuses have been tucked under the ivy to avoid looking too straight; this is achieved by sticking down the crocuses first and placing the ivy leaves slightly overlapping the crocus stems, a technique known as overlaying. Leave work to dry out before attempting to clean off any excess glue from the background and the paper decoration. Care should be taken when varnishing because the varnish is likely to collect around the edge of the tray where the base meets the sides. Brush the varnish on the inner sides first, before varnishing the base of the tray. Varnish the outside edge of the tray until it is the same color.*

◆

• materials list •

TWO OR MORE BOTTLE COASTERS
PREPARATION
Medium-grade sandpaper
PAINTING
Small can of white acrylic primer
1 inch (2.5cm) brush
Small can of primrose-yellow latex paint **or** small
  can white semigloss latex paint (if a paint finish
  is to be applied)
Materials for paint finish if required (see
  page 19)
DÉCOUPAGE
Wrapping paper illustrated with spring flowers (the
  one shown here is by Sandra Wall-Armitage)
Small sharp scissors   •   Craft knife
Wallpaper adhesive   •   Glue brush
Pasting board
Small sponge or paper towels
ANTIQUE GOLD
Small tubes of gold and raw umber artists'
  acrylics
No. 4 or 5 artist's brush
Lidded container or jar   •   Water to mix
VARNISHING
Tack cloth
Small can of satin polyurethane varnish or
  shellac
1 inch (2.5cm) brush
Fine-grade sandpaper   •   Mineral spirits
FINAL TOUCHES
Small piece of soft green self-adhesive baize or
  felt
Kitchen scissors

• preparation •

1 Rub the edges and surface of the coaster(s) with medium-grade sandpaper. Remove dust, apply first coat of primer and let it dry. Sand the coaster(s) again until smooth. Remove dust and paint on a second coat. Leave to dry.
2 Paint the coaster with two coats of yellow latex paint, letting it dry between coats.

• optional paint finishes •

Prepare as above, using a white semigloss latex topcoat instead of yellow. Then apply either a yellow or three-color sponged finish, as described above, right.

Yellow sponged finish Mix a paint glaze using one tablespoon of yellow paint, one tablespoon of polyvinyl white glue, and two or three tablespoons of water. Using the tip of a natural sponge, sponge on the glaze with light dabbing movements over the entire surface and let it dry.

Three-color sponging Mix a glaze using one tablespoon of the white semigloss latex paint used for the topcoat, one tablespoon of polyvinyl white glue, and two or three tablespoons of water.

Using the lid as a palette, squeeze out small amounts of yellow ocher, acid yellow and Chinese white artists' acrylics (or latex paints of those colors – measure with a spoon if using latex paint). Dip the sponge in the glaze first, before touching one or more of the colors with the tip. Sponge on diagonally, building up the color gradually. Let it dry. The inside of the coaster(s) may be painted in a contrasting color; for example, leaf-green.

• découpage •

1 Choose your favorite spring flowers, and cut them into tiny sprigs and flower heads. Turn each paper cutout face down on the pasting board and brush the glue evenly over the surface, making sure the edges are covered. Place the cutout into position, press air bubbles and excess glue out to the edges, and wipe away with a paper towel. When the flowers are flat, press the edges down. A craft knife is useful for lifting small cutouts. Apply to each facet of the coaster, and allow to dry thoroughly.
2 Choose a pretty central motif for the inside of the coaster. Apply as above and allow to dry.
3 Clean the surface of the work with a damp sponge or a paper towel, and leave to dry.

• finishing •

Apply an antique gold finish to the rim or molding of the coaster, as described on page 13. When dry, varnish as described on pages 13–14, taking care that the varnish doesn't run on the edges of the octagon. Varnish the inside also.

• final touches •

Mark out the shape of the coaster onto the paper backing of some self-adhesive baize or felt, and cut to fit the base of the coaster. This provides a professional finish and also protects furniture.

NESTLING IN THE GRASS *against the foot of a country fence is an early nineteenth-century tin hatbox, decorated with roses on a powder-blue painted background.*

◆

EDWARDIAN-STYLE PICNIC ITEMS

Inspiration for the blue work came while walking my dogs through the bluebell woods which surround my home. The beauty and vibrance of these simple wild flowers spreading in a soft carpet through the trees was enchanting, their color becoming almost fluorescent in the fading evening light. I came to a place in the woods where a young, windblown wild cherry sapling had become intertwined with ivy, forming a natural bower, and I began to imagine a romantic Edwardian picnic in this particularly lovely spot. Having finished their meal, my fantasy couple have wandered deeper into the woods, leaving their things behind – what a lovely thought. And how the mind wanders. The very simple pieces incorporated in the picnic are dealt with in the following pages.
(Isn't the parasol gorgeous?)
The cookie canister has been painted midnight blue, and given a simple design of hydrangeas in shades of blue and green which mingle beautifully with the background; very simple to cut. The waisted jug has another basic design of full white hyacinths and an iris. The little milk can (opposite), the old funnel and the Edwardian jug on page 51, were all found in local secondhand stores, and were prepared using a brighter blue paint for the background color. The step-by-step instructions are applicable to each item.

SOFT BLUES *and greens in the hydrangeas blend into the midnight-blue background of this cookie canister.*

(Opposite) A FANTASY *Edwardian picnic in an enchanted bluebell forest.*

• *materials list* •

VARIOUS EDWARDIAN-STYLE PICNIC ITEMS

PREPARATION
Red oxide metal primer
An old 1 inch (2.5cm) brush
Mineral spirits
Paper towels

PAINTING
Small can of midnight (or navy) blue flat latex
   paint
1 inch (2.5cm) brush

DÉCOUPAGE
Good-quality wrapping paper
Small sharp scissors
Craft knife
Wallpaper adhesive
Glue brush
Pasting board
Small sponge or paper towels

ANTIQUE GOLD
Small tubes of gold and raw umber artists'
   acrylics
No. 4 artist's brush
Lidded container or jar
Water to mix

VARNISHING
Tack cloth
Small can of satin polyurethane varnish or
   shellac
1 inch (2.5cm) brush

• *preparation* •

1   Prepare each item as described on pages 15–18. If the item is to be functional, do not apply red oxide primer to the inner surfaces.

2   When the red oxide metal primer is completely dry, apply at least three coats of dark blue latex paint – it is water based and fast drying. Allow each coat to dry before applying the next. The dark blue finish should look perfect and dense. Remember to turn the item upside down to paint the base.

• *découpage* •

1   Choose a few of the loveliest blooms and cut them out. You may find it easier to hold the base of the item in your lap while you are trying out different designs.

2   When you have selected the cutouts you wish to use, turn each one face down on the pasting board and spread the adhesive evenly over the entire surface, making sure the edges are covered. Turn right side up using a craft knife and apply to the item. Work out air bubbles, blemishes, and excess glue with your fingers, and when the paper is flat, press down the edges. Wipe away glue with damp paper towels. Allow to dry.

3   Clean up the surface of the work with a small damp sponge, working from the center of the design outward, and cleaning the background at the same time. Leave to dry.

• *finishing* •

Apply an antique gold finish to the container rims, as described on page 13. Leave to dry, then varnish as described on pages 13–14.

► *COOL WHITE snowdrops decorate small items painted in deep blue. The items look good painted in dark Chinese blue with a delicate but clear design in the snowdrops. I hand-painted the lovely old bellied jug in the picture with acrylics, and filled it with the darkest bluebells that I could find to complement the painting. Assembled on a crisp, white antique cloth, the white reflected in the wild wreath of fresh clematis on the wall behind completes the blue and white theme.*

CAMEO BOX AND CANDLESTICK

Having been an admirer of fine porcelain for many years, and a collector of English porcelain for a few, I began to look closely at the decoration on particular pieces. So often the flowers are hand-painted on a white background within a gilded "frame" which is surrounded by another color, like a cameo. Many plates are decorated in this way, and I thought it would be fun to transpose the idea onto a couple of small items using découpage instead of hand-painting.

♦

♦ *materials list* ♦

SMALL WOODEN BOX AND CANDLESTICK

PREPARATION

Fine-grade sandpaper

PAINTING

Small can of white acrylic primer

Small can of bright mid- or turquoise blue flat
    latex paint

1 inch (2.5cm) brush, or smaller

CAMEO WORK

White acrylic primer, as above

Small can of ivory or pale cream latex paint

No. 4 artist's brush

Piece of white chalk

ANTIQUE GOLD

Small tubes of gold and raw umber artists'
    acrylics

No. 4 artist's brush

Lidded container or jar

Water to mix

DÉCOUPAGE

Good-quality wrapping paper with tiny blooms

Small sharp scissors

Craft knife

Wallpaper paste

Glue brush

Pasting board

Small sponge or paper towels

VARNISHING

Tack cloth

Small can of satin or gloss polyurethane varnish
    or shellac

1 inch (2.5cm) brush, or smaller

FINAL TOUCHES

Small piece of self-adhesive baize or felt

Kitchen scissors

♦ *preparation* ♦

1   Sand the entire box using fine-grade sandpaper until smooth. Sand the candlestick by holding the sandpaper in the palm of your hand and working around it from top to bottom. Remove dust and apply two or three coats of white acrylic primer until the finish is perfect, allowing it to dry between coats.

2   Paint both items blue, applying at least two coats for

◄ *DÉCOUPAGE imitates antique porcelain.*

good allover cover, and leave to dry.

3   Draw the cameos with white chalk; this will allow mistakes to be removed easily until the cameos are the right shape and evenly spaced.

4   Block in the shapes with acrylic primer, allowing it to dry between coats. There should be no blue showing through. Apply two or three coats of the ivory or pale cream latex paint. All the paint is water based and will dry quickly, so this is not the lengthy procedure it seems.

5   Outline the cameos in antique gold (see page 13). Mix a portion of the color with a little water and hand-paint a faint thin line to the edges of the white. Balance the shape up as you go along – this can be done by widening the line or adding little dots, a rope design, or anything you find easy to apply. (Refer to pages 22–5 for hand-painted touches.)

6   When the cameos are dry and you are satisfied with their shape, paint one or two of the candlestick molding bands gold for a more decorative look. Leave to dry.

♦ *découpage* ♦

1   Cut a few of the smallest flowers and buds to fit within the shapes.

2   Turn each paper cutout face down onto the pasting board, and brush the paste evenly over the surface and over the edges. Turn right side up using a craft knife and apply to the surface. Work out air and excess glue with your fingers, and press down edges. Leave to dry out.

3   Clean off excess glue from the paper and the background with a dampened sponge or paper towel. Leave to dry. Remove dust with a tack cloth in preparation for varnishing.

♦ *finishing* ♦

Varnish the pieces as described on pages 13–14. Brush varnish out of the moldings on the candlestick where it will collect and yellow.

♦ *final touches* ♦

Cut out suitably sized pieces of self-adhesive baize, and attach to the undersides of both box and candlestick.

5

VIBRANT WORK

*F*or the first three projects in this chapter I have used papers designed and hand-painted by Sandra Wall-Armitage, which are marvelously bright and vibrant in color, the tulips and iris in particular. The blossom paper provides a true test of cutting and is very definitely advanced découpage! The lovely sweet-pea paper (origin unknown) was wrapped around a birthday gift. The tulip paper provides a wonderful splash of color on any background and, if used with a little flair, the flowers really come to life.

◆ ◆ ◆ ◆

BRILLIANTLY COLORED
tulips cut with a little
imagination look wonderful
on almost any background.

◆

Tumultuous Tulips – Jug and Box

This design is bright and cheerful, and would look super in a modern setting or as a focal point in a plainly decorated room. Both the jug and box are old; the deedbox dates back to the mid-nineteenth century and the jug is probably 1940s, but given the same treatment this is no longer apparent.
The lovely warm cream background provides a good neutral base on which to show up the brilliant colors of the tulips to their best advantage (black looks stunning, too.) The paper needs to be used imaginatively. By tucking short stems underneath the preceding row of flower heads and cutting extra stems to balance them, a natural effect will emerge. Sometimes they appear to be swaying in the breeze.

• materials list •

TINWARE JUG AND BOX
PREPARATION
Red oxide metal primer
An old 1 inch (2.5cm) brush
Mineral spirits
Paper towels
PAINTING
Small can of white acrylic primer
Small can of warm cream flat or semigloss latex
  paint
1 inch (2.5cm) brush
DÉCOUPAGE
Brightly colored paper with tulip design
Small sharp scissors
Craft knife
Wallpaper adhesive

Glue brush • Pasting board
Small sponge or paper towels
ANTIQUE GOLD
Small tubes of gold and raw umber artists'
  acrylics
No. 4 artist's brush
Lidded container or jar
Water to mix
VARNISHING
Tack cloth
Small can of satin shellac or varnish
1 inch (2.5cm) brush
FINAL TOUCHES
Suitably sized piece of self-adhesive baize or
  felt for base of box
Kitchen scissors

• preparation •

1 Prepare the items as described on pages 15–18.
2 When the red oxide metal primer is completely dry, apply at least two coats of white acrylic primer, allowing the first coat to dry before applying the second. It may be necessary to paint a third coat.
3 For the topcoat, apply two coats of warm cream flat or semigloss latex paint.

• découpage •

1 Cut out blocks of flowers, leaves, and stems, removing all unnecessary background. Lay the flowers on a sheet of white paper or a tabletop to get an idea of the type of design you would like to make.
2 Begin by pasting and sticking the underneath pieces first. A craft knife is useful for lifting small pasted cutouts from the pasting board. Reshape where necessary, and cut extra stems and leaves for a logical balanced design.
3 When the design is completed, leave to dry thoroughly before cleaning off the excess glue with a dampened sponge or paper towel.

• finishing •

Apply an antique gold finish to the rim of the jug, the rim of the box lid, and base, and the box's handles and escutcheon, as described on page 13. Leave to dry, then varnish as described on pages 13–14. Prop the lid of the box open to avoid sticking.

• final touches •

It is a good idea to attach some self-adhesive baize or felt to the underside of the box to protect your furniture from damage.

BLUE IRIS MILK CAN

A disused milk can has been painted an eye-catching bright blue and decorated with huge irises which appear to be "growing" from its base. It would look fantastic filled with walking sticks and umbrellas in a dark hall, or, with its lid replaced, as a pedestal for a jardiniere to display a wonderful arrangement of flowers. A thoroughly conspicuous, attractive, and unusual piece.

Many farmers will gladly sell their milk cans, now made redundant by milk tankers. Check first that they actually have a base, that the lid will come off, and that the whole thing isn't eaten away with rust. The more recent aluminum ones, like this one, do not have the character of the old pitted iron cans embossed with the farmer's name or that of the dairy, but are well worth decorating.

◆ materials list ◆

MILK CAN

PREPARATION
Wire brush if the can is rusty
Red oxide metal primer
An old 1 inch (2.5cm) brush
Mineral spirits
Paper towels

PAINTING
Small can of white acrylic primer
Small can of blue semigloss latex paint
    or color of your choice
1 inch (2.5cm) brush

DÉCOUPAGE
6 sheets of hand-painted paper with blue irises
    or other long-stemmed flowers

Small sharp scissors
Craft knife
Wallpaper adhesive
Pasting board   ◆   Glue brush
Small sponge or paper towels

HAND-PAINTED DECORATION
Either a small tube of artists' acrylic, or a small can
    of flat latex paint in a color of your choice to
    complement the topcoat
No. 5 artist's brush

VARNISHING
Tack cloth
Small can of pale satin shellac or varnish
1 inch (2.5cm) brush
Mineral spirits

◆ preparation ◆

1   Prepare the can as described on pages 15–18.
2   When the red oxide metal primer is completely dry, apply at least two coats of white acrylic primer, allowing the first coat to dry before applying the second.
3   Apply topcoat in a color of your choice. The can in the photograph has been painted in a lovely blue to complement the iris pattern.

◆ découpage ◆

1   The paper for this project has large motifs and is easy to cut, but the overall design has to be considered first and worked out carefully. The simplest method is to measure around the circumference of the base of the can, then transfer the measurement onto a tabletop. The cut flowers can be laid down on the table into a design. Where the design meets, extra filling-in may be neces-sary to tie the whole thing together. If possible, stand the can on the table to enable you to work at eye level and in a more comfortable position.
2   Paste and apply the cutouts, working out any excess glue or air bubbles from the center outward. A craft knife is helpful for lifting smaller cutouts.
3   Allow to dry thoroughly, then clean off the excess glue from the background and surface of the découpage using a damp sponge or paper towel.

◆ finishing ◆

Pick out the rim and handles in a complementary color using a No. 5 brush (violet has been used for the can illustrated). Leave to dry, then varnish as described on pages 13–14.

▶ *BLUE iris milk can.*

BLOSSOM BUCKETS

We continue the vibrant, springtime theme of the previous pages with a project involving very advanced cutting and pasting techniques. If you feel sufficiently confident to meet the challenge, find your sharpest, most pointed scissors and give it a try!
Filled to overflowing with wild flowers, which cover fields and roadsides in spring, or roses, lilacs, or blossoms of any kind, these buckets can be used for a floorstanding arrangement in a fireplace, in a corner, or perhaps on a hall table.
The blossom-covered paper was hand-painted by Sandra Wall-Armitage.

THE COLORS *are reversed on this galvanized bucket.*

BLOSSOM CASCADES *from the top of an Edwardian slop bucket.*

• materials list •

METAL BUCKET, ENAMELED IF POSSIBLE
PREPARATION
Red oxide metal primer
An old 1 inch (2.5cm) brush
Mineral spirits
Paper towels
PAINTING
Small can of white acrylic primer
Small can of white or lime-green semigloss latex
   paint for the topcoat
Small can of white or bright acid green latex
   paint for the sponging
1 inch (2.5cm) brush
Small natural sponge
DÉCOUPAGE
Blossom-covered paper (the one shown was
   hand-painted by Sandra Wall-Armitage)
Small sharp scissors
Craft knife
Wallpaper adhesive
Glue brush
Pasting board
Small sponge
HAND-PAINTED DECORATION
Small tubes of gold and raw umber artists'
   acrylics **or** a darker green paint could be used
   instead
Lidded container or jar
Water to mix
VARNISHING
Tack cloth
Small can of the palest satin shellac
1 inch (2.5cm) brush

• preparation •

1   Prepare the bucket as described on pages 15–18. For galvanized items see page 18.

2   When the red oxide metal primer is completely dry, apply three coats of white acrylic primer, allowing each coat to dry before applying the next.

3   Apply two or more coats of your chosen top color until the finish is perfect (allow to dry between coats).

4   A sponged-on finish should now be applied. You could follow the description on page 20, but I was extremely lazy with the sponging and in each case I dipped the tip of a dampened sponge directly into the can of paint (acid green sponged on the white bucket, and white sponged on the green bucket). The pattern of the sponging took the shape of wisteria or lilac cascading down from the rim of the bucket – as does the découpage design. The inside of each bucket has been sponged from the top rim, also quite sparsely. Allow to dry.

• découpage •

1   This is very advanced cutting, but the results, as you see, are very rewarding. Cut out blocks of leaves and blossom that would naturally hang downward. For the minutely detailed cutting out in between petals, make an incision with the pointed tip of one of the scissor blades first. If a stem is particularly difficult (and many are), cut straight through it and butt it together when you paste it on.

2   Paste evenly over the back of the cutout pieces, taking the glue over the edges onto the pasting board. If this proves too difficult, you could, as an alternative, apply the glue to the surface of the bucket. Use a craft knife to assist in removing the cutouts from the pasting board and to position them on the bucket. (It is a good idea to rinse the glue from your fingers every so often, otherwise the surface of the paper will come off.)

3   A few of the larger leaves can be arranged around the top rim of the bucket last of all, to help balance the design and to give the impression of hanging foliage. Small leaf decorations can be stuck inside the top rim of the bucket to finish it off.

4   When all the design is stuck on, leave it to dry out before cleaning off the excess glue from the work with a damp sponge or paper towel.

• finishing •

Apply an antique gold finish to the handle, rim, and base of the bucket, as described on page 13. On a green bucket you may prefer to pick out the features with a darker leaf-green paint. Allow to dry, then varnish as described on pages 13–14.

(Overleaf) THE EDWARDIAN *handled bucket is sponged a fresh new-leaf-green onto a white background to make a perfect backdrop for the design of lilac and apple blossom. Inside are a few ivy leaves. The second bucket is of the modern galvanized variety and more squat in shape, but treated in a reverse paint effect (i.e. green background with white sponging) and finished in green rather than gilded. They make a pretty pair!*

LETTER HOLDER

HAND-PAINTED LETTER HOLDER *Hand-colored photocopies may be used instead of wrapping paper for the découpage design. This letter holder was decorated with photocopied line drawings, which were cut out and pasted on. When dry, they were hand-painted with acrylics used thickly like oil paint. This is an easy and quick way of decorating small items. (For suppliers of such items, see page 142.)*

Sweet Pea Cachepot and Box

This cachepot makes an attractive holder for one or more flower pots, which will brighten any kitchen or sunroom. The materials required for the tin box are exactly the same as for the cachepot, and the sweet pea design is applied in almost the same way. A grouping of blooms has been applied to the lid top in the shape of an oval. The rims, keyhole, and handles have been gilded, and the underneath baized.

• materials list •

METAL CACHEPOT

PREPARATION
Red oxide metal primer
An old 1 inch (2.5cm) brush
Mineral spirits
Paper towels

PAINTING
Small can of white acrylic primer
Small cans of soft green and pale blue flat latex paint (or a slate color)
1 inch (2.5cm) brush

DÉCOUPAGE
Paper depicting sweet peas
Small sharp scissors
Craft knife
Wallpaper adhesive
Glue brush
Pasting board
Small sponge or paper towels

ANTIQUE GOLD
Small tubes of gold and raw umber artists' acrylics
No. 4 artist's brush
Lidded container or jar
Water to mix

VARNISHING
Tack cloth
Small can of satin shellac or varnish
1 inch (2.5cm) brush

• preparation •

1 Prepare tinware as described on pages 15–18. For zinc or galvanized items, see page 18.
2 When the red oxide is completely dry, apply at least two coats of white acylic primer, allowing it to dry between coats.
3 For the top coat, apply two coats of a soft slate color

(or soft blue and green painted on with one brush, dipping it first into blue and then into green without cleaning), taking care over the handles and the scalloped edge where the paint will collect and run both inside and out.

• découpage •

1 Cut out the curling stems with care, because their shape and form will enhance the decoration. If you find them difficult to handle – especially to paste – the stems can be cut at intervals and butted together when they are stuck on the cachepot.
2 Turn each cutout face down on the pasting board and brush on the paste evenly making sure the edges are covered. Turn right side up using the craft knife and position on the cachepot. (Don't panic if a design curls up, just uncurl it gently.)
3 When the decoration is finished, leave it to dry out. Clean the excess glue from the background and the surface of the decoration, working carefully with a damp sponge or paper towel.

• finishing •

Apply an antique gold finish to the scalloped edge of the cachepot, as described on page 13 – remember to neaten the inside, too. Leave to dry. Paint the bottom rim and the handles in the same way, and allow to dry. Finally, varnish as described on pages 13–14. Brush out any runs on the scalloped edge and where the handles join the body of the cachepot. Approximately 10 coats should be sufficient for the outside and, unless there is a great difference in the color, two or three coats should be enough for the inside.

(Overleaf) SWEET PEA CACHEPOT *A pretty summery decoration of sweet peas entwines its way around a fluted cachepot. The background is streaked in two colors of flat latex paint: a soft green and a pale blue combine in places to make a lovely aquamarine. The box has a similar decoration.*

6
FURNITURE

It is very rewarding to transform a shabby piece of furniture completely. One sometimes hears of suitable pieces languishing at the back of a garage or garden shed, stored in a barn, or occasionally thrown out! They may have had a little woodworm or damage, or possibly have become unfashionable. Auctions, antiques stores and flea markets are another source of secondhand furniture ripe for simple restoration. Stripping is sometimes necessary, but often only painting is needed. Don't dismiss reproduction pieces because they can be made to look old and antique; the main criterion is a good shape.

• • • •

VICTORIAN PINE CUPBOARD

A good old country cupboard, which would have originated as a wall cupboard in a large high-ceilinged Victorian kitchen. The body of the cupboard is painted in a bright leaf-green latex paint, and the front and side panels have been sponged in three colors in a diagonal flowing movement. The découpage decoration has been "mirrored" on the two panels. This idea could be used on closet doors in the right setting.

• materials list •	
DOUBLE-DOORED WOODEN CUPBOARD	Small sharp scissors • Craft knife
PREPARATION	Wallpaper paste • Glue brush
Medium-grade sandpaper	Pasting boards • Piece of white chalk
PAINTING	Tape measure • Small sponge or paper towels
White acrylic primer	**HAND-PAINTED DECORATION**
1 inch (2.5cm) brush	Small tube of Venetian red artists' acrylic
Small can of leaf-green latex paint	No. 8 artist's brush • Water to mix
Small can of white semigloss latex paint	**VARNISHING**
Small can of palest gray flat latex paint	Small can of satin polyurethane varnish or
Small tube of Payne's gray artists' acrylic (optional)	shellac
Polyvinyl white glue	1 inch (2.5cm) brush • Tack cloth
Lidded container and small carton	Fine-grade sandpaper • Mineral spirits
Natural sponge	**TO POLISH THE CUPBOARD**
DÉCOUPAGE	Natural beeswax or white beeswax polish and soft
6 sheets of good-quality wrapping paper	cloth (see page 83)

▶ *HUGE ROSES adorn an old Victorian cupboard. I hand-painted the old Victorian hatbox with wild roses; it fits well into the charming setting of a rose-covered patio at the home of a friend.*

◆

◆ *preparation* ◆

1 If your cupboard is of stripped wood, prepare it by sanding thoroughly in the same direction as the grain. If your piece is painted or stained, treat as described on pages 14–15.

2 Remove dust; apply the first coat of primer and let it dry. Run your hand over the surface and edges, and if there are rough patches remaining, rub it down again. When you are satisfied the surface is smooth to the touch, apply the second coat and let it dry. Paint the cupboard with two or three coats until the surface looks near perfect in its prime coat.

3 Topcoat with two or three coats of leaf-green latex paint, remembering to leave the side and door panels white. Leave to dry.

4 Apply two coats of white semigloss latex paint to the panels and let them dry.

5 Mix one tablespoon of the leaf-green latex paint with sufficient white semigloss latex to lighten the green. Then mix a paint glaze by combining one tablespoon of Polyvinyl white glue, one tablespoon of the paler green paint mix, and approximately three tablespoons of water. On the lid place a little pale gray flat latex, a portion of white semigloss latex, and a small squeeze of Payne's gray.

6 Squeeze the natural sponge out in clean water and remove excess moisture. Dip the tip of the sponge into the green glaze, and with light dabbing movements work at an angle, diagonally, leaving two or three spaces in which to sponge on the soft gray. Leave to dry. For the second sponging, the green can be built up a little more and white added to the sponge in some places, and a touch of Payne's gray for added interest. When you are happy with the finish, add the lines of soft gray and leave it all to dry completely.

◆ *découpage* ◆

1 Cut out a selection of lovely large blooms, some with buds and interesting stamens, fine curling stems, thorns; a good variety will add interest and depth to the design.

Have plenty of leaves to look as natural as possible, and aim to choose colors which will blend with the background or the overall color scheme.

2 A low cupboard can be laid on its back to make designing easier, but assuming the cupboard is upright, cut for one door only and decorate it first. It might be helpful to hold the cutouts against the panel and mark their outlines with chalk.

3 Turn each cutout face down on the board and paste evenly all over, making sure the edges are covered. Using a craft knife, turn right side up and position on the panel, taking extra care to work out air bubbles and excess glue which is always a problem with large flowers. Press from the center outward with a rolling finger movement, wiping the glue away with damp paper towels. **Stand back and look** occasionally, because it is impossible to see the overall design when you are right on top of it.

4 Before decorating the second door panel, it is a good idea to measure the margins around the design and where the largest and most noticeable blooms are. Chalk around the shapes again to help position the cutouts correctly. You will have to dissect the flowers and leaves, and reshape them, in order for them to appear as a mirror image. It will be necessary to fill in with the odd leaf and bud to balance the picture.

5 When both panels are finished, allow the work to dry out before cleaning off the excess glue from the background and the decoration with a damp sponge.

◆ *finishing* ◆

Mix a small amount of Venetian red with a little water, and draw a steady straight line around the inside edge of the panels. Keep some damp paper towels by your side to wipe off smudges and mistakes. Allow to dry completely, then varnish the panels as described on pages 13–14. Apply at least 10 coats.

(*NOTE* It is not necessary to varnish the frame, because latex can be wax polished to a satin-like patina using a soft cloth. Do this only when the varnish is completely dry.)

COMMODE

COMMODE *Made of oak, this little commode was found in an antiques and secondhand store. I
thought it would be fun to decorate it as a box to use with the lid open to display flowers.
The commode was rubbed down with medium-grade sandpaper, the rotten wood by the old hinges
was repaired and filled, and new hinges were fitted. It was first given two coats of flat varnish to
stop the dark stain bleeding into the paint, then painted in dark red latex paint and "streaked" to
add depth and interest, by brushing Payne's gray acrylic over the wet red latex and leaving the brush
marks. The découpage decoration is cut from another favorite paper, and the mixture of fruit and
flowers is a little different. For the front panel I used vine leaves from another paper to give a three-
dimensional look. The little hand-painted leaves on the top balance the design. The decoration is
under approximately 15 coats of varnish.*

◆

♦

DEMI-LUNE TABLE

The elegant lines of this pretty little table have been accentuated by the display of two tall candlestick lamps and a profusion of pink roses underneath an antique mirror, making a most attractive feature in a hall which can be tucked into the smallest space.
It is a reproduction which has been decorated to look like an old table. The cameo effect is simple to do with two colors of paint and a steady hand. The delicate floral decoration is découpage and requires some meticulously fine cutting, although different flowers could be chosen. The table has been aged with an antique and craquelure finish.

• materials list •

DEMI-LUNE TABLE
PREPARATION
Medium-grade sandpaper
PAINTING
White acrylic primer
1 inch (2.5cm) brush
Small can of gardenia or cream semigloss latex paint
Small can of soft green latex paint (or color of your choice)
No. 4 artist's brush
DÉCOUPAGE
Good-quality paper covered in tiny delicate flowers
Small sharp scissors
Craft knife
Wallpaper adhesive
Glue brush
Pasting board
Small sponge or paper towels
HAND-PAINTED DECORATION
Small tubes of gold and raw umber artists' acrylics
No. 3 or 4 lining brush
Lidded jar or container
Water to mix
VARNISHING
Tack cloth
Small can of satin polyurethane varnish or shellac
1 inch (2.5cm) brush
Fine-grade sandpaper
Mineral spirits
CRAQUELURE
Materials as listed on page 25

• preparation •

1   Sand the table if necessary to provide a "key" for the paint. Apply two or three coats of fast-drying acrylic primer, allowing each coat to dry before applying the next. Wash brush thoroughly in soap and water to use again for the topcoat.
2   Apply at least two coats of gardenia or cream semigloss latex paint for a good allover cover to all surfaces except the front panels. It is often a good idea to turn the table upside down to begin, painting as much as possible before turning it back the right way up to complete the coat of paint. Leave to dry.
3   Paint the front panels in soft green latex paint.
4   Mark out faintly the shape of the cameos onto the top and front of the table, using very pale, weak green paint.

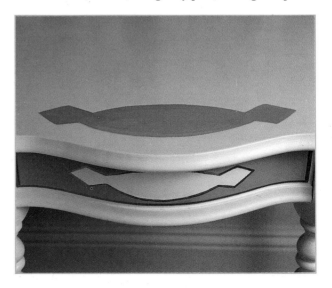

CAMEO shapes before outlining.

► *PAINTING and découpage combine to decorate an elegant demi-lune table.*

♦

Mistakes can be wiped off using dampened paper towels. You may have to try several times to get the shape right, but this is quite usual. (Alternatively, you could trace the shape below as a guideline.)

5   Paint the cameo shapes with an art brush. You will require a few coats to get a solid color; don't worry if the edges are not perfect, they can be improved when the cameo is outlined. Have a piece of paper towel handy to erase mistakes.

6   Now line the cameos using antique gold, mixed as described on page 13. Cover the lining brush evenly without overloading it. Place the tip of the brush on the beginning of a line and pull the brush toward you; when the paint runs out, replenish and continue with the outline. Take care to replace the tip of the brush onto the gold line, overlapping a little. Remove mistakes and smudges quickly with damp paper towels.

• *découpage* •

1   The choice of design is yours; small posies or a centrally positioned group of tiny blooms would look just as attractive as the delicate flowers and stems used in the photograph. Cut out a good selection, paying great attention to detail and accuracy. Begin by placing the cutouts on the tabletop to fill in the three cameos until they look balanced. Stand back and look. If your design is positioned centrally, chalk around the edges of the cutouts which will be helpful when they are replaced

after pasting. The fine stemmy design was pasted on in sections without the aid of chalk marks because they would have been thicker than the stems themselves.

2   To paste, turn each cutout face down on the board and brush the glue evenly over the surface, making sure that the edges are covered. Use a craft knife to ease the fragile cutouts gently from the board and to position them on the table. Rinse your fingers occasionally to avoid taking the surface off the paper. Press the cutouts down when all the blemishes have been removed. When the decoration is complete, leave to dry.

3   When all three cameos on the top of the table have been completed, check that they look balanced. If not, fill in any gaps by adding the odd leaf or stem until it is attractive to the eye. Decorate the remainder in exactly the same way. Leave to dry out.

4   Clean up the work carefully, using either a slightly dampened sponge or paper towels. Should any fine stem become loose or dislodged, restick it. Remove all excess glue from the surface of the table with the sponge or paper towel so it is perfectly clean and free from dust. The table is now ready to varnish.

• *finishing* •

Because the table is to have an antique and craquelure finish, apply a thin coat of varnish *to the cameos only*, to seal the paper cutouts. Leave to dry. Apply the craquelure and aging varnish as described on pages 25–6.

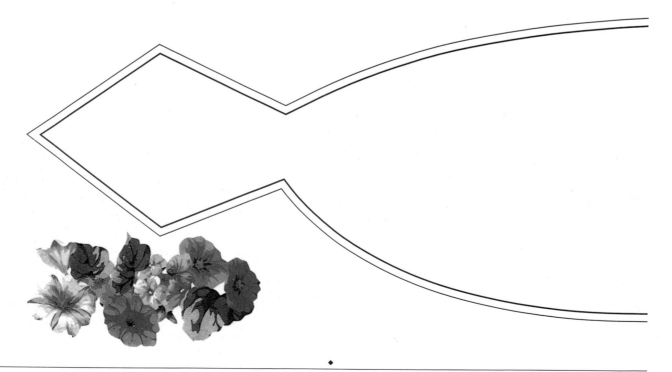

◆

CAMEOS *outlined in antique
gold frame the finely cut
flowers.*

TRACE *the cameo shapes onto
the table using the pattern
provided.*

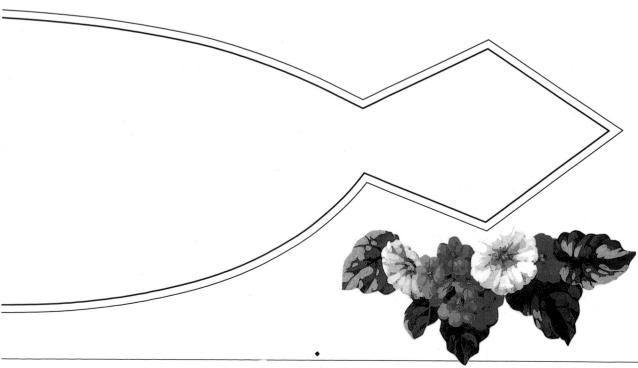

◆

FLORENTINE DESK AND BALLOON-BACK CHAIR

Both the oak desk and the Victorian balloon-back chair were bought cheaply at auctions. The desk was in very poor condition, having many gouges and cuts which, to make matters worse, had been filled with plaster – quite unsuitable for wood. What a challenge!
The delicate balloon-back chair tucks into a corner of my small study and doubles as an extra occasional or dining-room chair when friends visit.
Both have been painted in black latex paint and decorated in a Florentine-design paper, taken from a seventeenth-century tabletop on which the grapes were mother-of-pearl.

• materials list •

DESK AND CHAIR

PREPARATION

Medium-grade sandpaper (use a coarser sandpaper for hard oak only)

Fine-grade sandpaper

Very fine-grade sandpaper

Sanding block

Soft cloth

Water-based wood spackle

Putty knife

Small can of natural beeswax or antique furniture polish, and soft cloth to apply (if drawers should not run freely)

PAINTING

Pint (liter) can of black flat latex paint

1 inch (2.5cm) brush

DÉCOUPAGE

8 sheets of Florentine wrapping paper

Small sharp scissors

Craft knife

Wallpaper adhesive

Small glue brush • Pasting board

Small sponge or paper towels

Piece of white chalk

ANTIQUE GOLD

Small tubes of gold and raw umber artists' acrylics

No. 5 artist's brush

Lidded container or jar

Water to mix

VARNISHING

Tack cloth

Small can of satin polyurethane varnish or shellac

1 inch (2.5cm) brush

Fine-grade sandpaper

Mineral spirits

TO POLISH THE DESK AND CHAIR

Natural beeswax, white beeswax, or antique furniture polish, and a soft cloth; see page 83

► *A RUSTIC OAK desk and Victorian balloon-back chair decorated as a pair for a small study.*

♦ *preparing the desk* ♦

If your piece is painted, you may find the services of a professional furniture-stripping company, who often collect and deliver, well worthwhile for the amount of effort it saves. If you tackle the job yourself, an electric power sander will cut your work in half, but there is no reason why most pieces cannot be done by hand. If your furniture is painted, please turn to page 15 for preparation of wood.

1   Remove all handles and decorative fixtures, if possible, and remove the drawers. Clean off any damaged leather or paper lining in the top of the desk by soaking it off with water. Fill chips, holes, and deep scratches in the wood with a water-based wood spackle or putty.

2a   **Hand sanding** Cut the abrasive sheet into quarters and wrap it around the sanding block. Do not fold the sheet into four, otherwise the abrasive surfaces will be facing one another and will wear out quickly. If you prefer, you may use the whole sheet with the flat of your hand, but it is more difficult to keep a grip. Sand your piece down, keeping an even pressure and always sanding in the same direction as the grain in the wood. Pay particular attention to the edges of the desk and those of the lid and drawers. When the surface begins to feel smooth to the touch, wipe it with a damp cloth following the grain to remove the dust and avoid clogging, and to raise the grain for the next sanding.

2b   **Power sanding** If you have an orbital sander you could use abrasive paper with a medium paper backing, but if it is a disc or drum sander, cloth-backed abrasive paper may last longer. Alternatively, the appropriate sandpaper can be used to fit your particular type of machine.

Always sand in the same direction as the grain in the wood, and pay particular attention to the edges of the desk and those of the drawers and the lid. It is worth smoothing the edges of drawers to protect fine articles which may be stored in them. When the surface is even, and all cuts and chips are removed, run your fingers over it. If it feels smooth, switch off the sander and wipe over the surface with a damp cloth to remove the dust and avoid clogging – this will also open up the grain for the next sanding.

3   Keep renewing the piece of sandpaper if you are using a sanding block, and knock it occasionally to avoid clogging. Take the fine-grade sandpaper and begin the whole process again, frequently running your hand over the wood to get a good indication of how it is progressing and where imperfections remain. When it is finished, remove the dust with a brush or damp cloth. The surface needs a "key" on which to paint, not a finished sanding.

4   Replace the drawers to see if they run smoothly; if they stick, a minor adjustment is necessary. Using very fine sandpaper, hand sand the top and bottom edges of the drawer(s) which should glide along the runners. With a soft cloth, apply a good measure of wax polish, rubbing the edges. Leave for five minutes, then sand the polish into the edges until the surface is satin smooth (this happens quickly). When the drawers are finished, leave them out of the frame for painting.

♦ *painting the desk* ♦

Because black is a difficult color to work on if the light is inadequate, use an angle-lamp or spotlight; otherwise it will be impossible to see into the small sections in the top of the desk. Remove debris and dust before you

apply the first coat of black latex paint. Paint the inside top and lid, and let it dry. Paint the frame and the drawer fronts, and leave to dry. Apply two or three more coats until the overall cover is good, and let it dry. Replace handles, lock, and escutcheons.

◆ *découpage* ◆

1 The Florentine paper is tricky to cut, but fortunately the background is the same color as the paint and if a little of the background remains it will not be noticeable. The curling stems and grapes can be cut out in sections, since they are fragile to paste and stick; they can then be butted together to form one continuous length when they are stuck to the surface of the desk.

2 Draw a faint chalk mark to indicate the shape and position of the design on the desk. Cut a good selection of grapes and fruit so you have plenty to choose from for the decoration.

3 To paste, turn each paper cutout face down on the board and brush the adhesive evenly over the surface. Use the craft knife to assist in lifting the cutout from the board and positioning on the desk. Once in place, press down flat. Fingers require frequent washing because the excess glue will build up and remove the surface of the paper.

4 When each section of the desk is decorated, leave it to dry out. **Stand back and look** occasionally to check if the design is balanced, equidistant from drawer handles, and so forth. Extra pieces can be cut to fill in where necessary.

5 The inside of the flap of the oak desk in the photograph was too chipped and uneven to decorate, but was masked by self-adhesive black suede fabric, which was neatened by adding a braided trim. The inside and top is decorated with fruit.

6 When the decoration is dry, clean up the surface and background to remove excess glue with a damp sponge or paper towel. Let it dry.

◆ *finishing* ◆

Remove dust with a tack cloth. Take the drawers out of the desk to avoid sticking. Apply varnish as described on pages 13–14, brushing it out evenly to avoid runs. Varnish both inside and out. When the final coat has dried, leave for 24 hours until the varnish has hardened. Apply beeswax polish, buffing with a soft cloth after 10 minutes. Repeat until a silky patina is achieved.

◆ *florentine chair* ◆

The balloon-back chair in the photograph is mahogany with a lot of nonactive worm holes (nothing will survive chemical stripping).

1 Turn the chair upside down on a working surface that is protected with a plastic sheet. Hand sand until smooth. Apply several coats of black paint, both in this position and afterward turning the chair upright. Let it dry between coats. Cut out a design of your choice, and decorate the back and front of the frame using the same technique as for the desk.

2 Because the chair is Victorian, it is in keeping with the style to decorate the pretty turned legs and spindle with antique gold, as described on page 13.

3 When the antique gold is dry, varnish carefully as before, applying only two coats to the lower parts, but at least 10 coats over the design on the front and back of the chair, since it will be constantly touched and must be hardwearing.

4 When the chair is absolutely dry, it can be upholstered, or re-covered quickly and easily by stretching a piece of muslin or silk over the seat and stapling it underneath with a staple gun.

7

THE LIVING ROOM

$\mathscr{A}$ room in which to relax and enjoy life's peaceful pleasures: good conversation, reading, music. During the winter months, it is an ideal place to gather around the fire for afternoon tea or to entertain friends in the evening. Why not make the coffee table (below) or screen (page 90) a special feature of the room? Decorated in an outstandingly beautiful design, it will give you lasting pleasure.

• • • •

COFFEE TABLE

This table is one of the most admired pieces of work I have ever produced. It literally stopped people in their tracks as they were passing my stand at the Country Living Fair in London, all enchanted by the huge full-blown roses on a sumptuous background which give it such a lifelike vibrance. One can almost touch the flowers and breathe in their scent. This is a fine example of the potential of paint finishes, the use of color and the versatility of découpage design.

This table is constructed from new pine with a medium-density fiberboard top, which is a perfect surface on which to work. Many similar pieces are available from furniture stores and by mail-order. It has been paint-finished to look like polished slate using the technique of three-color sponging.

Another option would be to use a rich Chinese red and decorate with bold flowers taken from a print of a Dutch masters painting, then apply an antique and craquelure finish (see pages 25–6) and gild fairly heavily (see page 13). Alternatively, paint black and decorate using a paper depicting the finest seventeenth-century Florentine design to make a border on the tabletop, applying many coats of varnish to make the grapes shine like mother-of-pearl. All quite different and varied pieces of work, and just a few examples of what can be achieved.

The pictured design of full-blown summer roses is under at least 25 layers of varnish. After approximately 20 coats it was rubbed down with the finest grade of steel wool, the process being repeated between three or four subsequent coats in order to produce a good finish.

The table has been in constant use for three years and is polished regularly with white beeswax polish, which improves the patina and renews the "glow" and depth.

BUTTERFLIES AND BUGS *enhance the natural look of this flowered design.*

•

◆ materials list ◆

COFFEE TABLE

PREPARATION

1 sheet of medium-grade sandpaper (if the
   pine legs are rough) or fine-grade
   sandpaper

Very fine-grade sandpaper

PAINTING

Small can of white acrylic primer

Small can of semigloss latex paint in a bright
   strong blue

1 inch (2.5cm) brush

2 natural sponges (or one large one cut up)

Wide-necked plastic carton with lid

Old lids to use as palettes

Old spoon to measure paint

Container of clean water for washing sponges

Paper towels

Large tubes of white, Payne's gray, and
   Hooker's green artists' acrylics

Small tube of black artists' acrylic

Polyvinyl white glue

Water to mix

DÉCOUPAGE

Paper of your choice

Small sharp scissors

Craft knife

Wallpaper adhesive

Small glue brush

Pasting boards

Small sponge or paper towels

Piece of white chalk   ◆   Tack cloth

ANTIQUE GOLD

Tubes of gold and raw umber artists' acrylics

No. 5 artist's brush

Lidded container or jar   ◆   Water to mix

VARNISHING

Tack cloth

Quart (2 liter) can of clear gloss polyurethane
   varnish or shellac and smallest can of satin

1 inch (2.5cm) brush

Fine-grade sandpaper

Fine grade steel wool or very fine black "wet and
   dry" sandpaper

Mineral spirits

TO POLISH THE TABLE

Soft cloth

White beeswax polish

◆ preparation ◆

Preparation is particularly important to the success of this project, and time spent at this stage will be rewarded by the end result.

1 It is not uncommon for new pine in the raw to be rough, and therefore the legs may need sanding down with medium-grade sandpaper. Sand in the same direction as the grain, paying special attention to the edges. Change to fine-grade sandpaper for a finer finish, feeling the wood with your fingers and smoothing your hand over the surface to detect any further areas that need attention.

2 Feel the top surface and around the molding on the edges; if the particleboard feels rough, sand it with fine sandpaper. Remove dust and turn the table upside down onto a workbench or table (which can be protected with a plastic sheet) to save bending down.

3 Apply the first coat of white acrylic primer to the underside, legs, and anything else that is visible, and leave to dry. Turn the table upright and paint the remainder, working in the direction of the grain (because the top is particleboard, you will have to imagine that the grain would run the length of the surface). Take care not to clog up the molded edges. Leave to dry.

4 With a piece of very fine sandpaper, sand the table down again until it is smooth. You may find it easier to use a quarter of the sheet wrapped around a sanding block to work on the tabletop. Remove the dust, apply the second coat of acrylic primer, and leave to dry.

5 Continue along these lines until you are satisfied with the look and feel of the table, and a good allover cover has been achieved with the primer.

6 In the same way, but without sanding between coats, apply two or three coats of the bright blue semigloss latex paint for the topcoat which will receive the paint finish. Leave to dry.

7 In a container, measure out two tablespoons of bright blue paint, two tablespoons of white glue, and between four and eight tablespoons of water. Mix together to make a glaze. On the lids, squeeze out a length of Payne's gray, Hooker's green and white with a smaller amount of black.

8 Squeeze the sponges out in clean water and dab off excess water on paper towels. With the first sponge, begin by dipping part of it into the blue paint glaze and part of it into the Payne's gray, and apply at random onto the surface, building up areas of color. Next try the blue glaze with some of the green and white, and so on, mainly working up from dark to light and working to cover quite a substantial part of the top of the table, sides and legs. Build up the colors until the sponges are full of paint and they will eventually begin to merge. Leave to dry out for a time and wash the sponges for the next attempt. Replenish the colors on the palette when necessary. Repeat the process and make alterations in the color as you go along; if the base color is dark, by using white with the dark colors and pressing the sponge quite hard, "depth" will begin to appear. Sponge the whole table, walking around it and standing back to look at it constantly to ensure complete coverage. When you are pleased with the result, leave it to dry for several hours. (See also page 20 for picture showing how to build up the colors for polished slate finish.)

You may need to rinse out the sponges once or twice, and your hands and nails will be covered in the glaze but this will clean off with soap and water. Remember to wash the sponges out finally in soap and water, and leave them in cold water to recover for a while.

◆ *découpage* ◆

1 Cut out several large blooms, a collection of buds, and interesting leaves, especially if they have dewdrops on them. Choose a few long sprays and curling delicate stems for balancing the design later on, and as many butterflies, bugs, and bees that you are able to lay your hands on. The design is overlaid quite a lot, so begin by placing the paper cutouts on the table surface, trying them in different positions until you have a balanced shape for the basis of the design. Remember to walk around the table because the picture must be attractive and balanced from each side. The larger flowers and leaves will look best forming the base of the design, with smaller flowers overlaid or filling in toward the top.

2 When you are quite satisfied, hold the design flat with the palm of your hand and chalk around the edge of the paper cutouts, marking their shape onto the table surface. As the design is overlaid, you will have to remove the uppermost cutouts to chalk around those underneath.

3 Turn each cutout face down onto the pasting board, brushing on the glue evenly over the surface and making sure the edges are covered. Use a craft knife to assist in turning the cutout right side up and position on the surface within the chalk marks. Because the flowers are large, it is important to take great care to remove all the excess glue and air bubbles, working from the center outward with a rolling movement of the fingers. Look at the work in an indirect light, which will highlight bubbles, creases, and blemishes. When the work is absolutely flat, press down the edges and wipe away excess glue with a damp sponge or paper towel while you are working. Continue in this way until the larger base flowers and leaves are in place, and you can begin to build up the design. Remember **to stand back and look** every now and then, because the shape and overall balance can not be appreciated when you are right on top of it. Gaps and unevenness will appear, and can be filled in with little extras cut specifically for the spaces. Keep checking that everything is pressed down flat; it really does need to be perfect on a tabletop.

4 When you are quite satisfied with the decoration, leave to dry out before cleaning up; the chalk marks will have almost disappeared, but the surface of the paper and background will be gluey. With a small sponge dampened with hot water, gently remove the excess glue from the surface of the design, taking care not to scuff the edges of the paper; clean the background and any remaining chalk marks. If any edges or stems rise up, they can be restuck, and left to dry.

◆ *finishing* ◆

Apply an antique gold finish around the moldings, as described on page 13. Take care when painting around the top edge of the table not to stray over onto the table-top. Have a piece of damp paper towel handy to wipe any smudges off in a flash should this occur, since the gold particles will be highlighted by the varnish. Leave to dry.

◆ *varnishing* ◆

Gloss varnish is used to build up a hardwearing surface, the last 2 or 3 coats only are satin. The varnishing stage is especially important in this project, and the following directions should be followed to the letter.

1 Take a tack cloth and remove every particle of dust from the legs, sides, moldings, and last of all remove the dust from the tabletop, working in one direction.

2 Using the clear gloss, apply a thin coat of varnish to the top; begin by brushing around the outside and filling in, spreading it on evenly to cover the entire surface. Wipe the brush on the edge of the can to remove the excess and, using the tip, brush over the varnished surface again, working in one direction. At the first sign of drying, tackiness, or spun-sugar look, STOP! Leave to dry.

Between coats, place the brush in a jar containing mineral spirits: mash it around a bit and leave until the next application. You should be able to apply a coat in the morning and another in the evening or late afternoon in the right environment. Varnish drying times will vary according to room temperature, but damp conditions should be avoided. At the end of each day, remove the excess varnish from the brush, mash vigorously in mineral spirits, wash out in soap and lukewarm water, and rinse thoroughly. Leave to dry in a dust-free place. If the mineral spirits shows any sign of clouding, throw it away.

Before each application, remove all mineral spirits from the brush. Then use a tack cloth to make sure all the dust has been removed from the surface of the table. Subsequent coats may be applied more generously – slurped or "floated" on, using the same method of spreading evenly over the surface, removing the excess frequently from the brush, brushing it in one direction only, almost taking the varnish off again until it is evenly spread out. By beginning around the outside and filling in, this gives you the chance to catch any runs that may spread or dribble over the molding edge, and reduces the possibility of the edges drying or becoming tacky before you have the chance to complete the process.

3   An absolute minimum of 10 coats (preferably more) must be applied before any bits of dust, hairs, or undulations can be removed by sanding gently with very fine sandpaper. Do not panic when fine white scratch marks appear, these will be covered by the next layer of varnish. Keep the sandpaper away from the edges, otherwise they will quickly show through. Take care not to scuff the edge or surface of the paper.

4   At this stage you may want to lift the table onto a working surface or tabletop to enable you to apply one or two coats to the legs and frame. Continue to apply varnish to the tabletop until the edges of the paper are no longer visible, and the decoration has taken on an almost three-dimensional depth – a glow. When this stage has been reached, probably after 20 coats, you can begin the final stages of rubbing down with black "wet and dry" very fine sandpaper used wet, or fine steel wool used dry (one steel-wooling might be all that is necessary). Remove dirty water with paper towels and wipe the surface clean. Let dry. Clean well with a tack cloth before applying the next layer of varnish.

5   Cut off a manageable piece of steel wool and, using it dry with *light* pressure and working in a circular motion, polish up the surface until smooth. Remove *all* steel wool particles and dust. Clean thoroughly with a tack cloth, and apply another slightly thinner coat of satin varnish to the surface. Leave to dry for 24 hours. Clean again and apply what will hopefully be the last coat of satin varnish, which should look as near perfect as possible. Leave to dry. Make sure the gloss varnish is entirely covered, otherwise apply another "last" coat. Let harden for two or three days.

YOU CAN ALMOST smell these sumptuous full-blown roses on a polished-slate paint-finished background.

◆ *polishing* ◆

Apply a generous coat of white beeswax polish on the tabletop in the same direction as the grain. Leave to dry for about 15 minutes, then buff and polish up the surface until it glows. Repeat this process several times over the next day or two, and the patina will be absolutely fabulous. Stand back and admire! Your beautiful, hardwearing table will be the cause of much admiration and will give you a great deal of pleasure.

◆

PARAVENT SCREEN

A most versatile decorative item, the little screen fulfills many roles; seen in the photograph as a pretty backdrop for a collection of treasured objets d'art *displayed on a circular table, it looks equally attractive in a fireplace facing either way since it is decorated on both sides. Useful for concealing an ugly radiator, or adding a touch of color and interest in a corner, or purely for decoration. The screen shown has panels 25 inches high × 14 inches wide (75 × 35cm). Similar screens may be found at antiques stores.*

• materials list •

PARAVENT SCREEN

PREPARATION
Medium- and very fine-grade sandpaper

PAINTING
Small can of white acrylic primer
Small can of gardenia (or other pale color)
   semigloss latex paint (for the panels)
Small can of slate-green (or similar) flat or
   semigloss latex paint (for the frame)
1 inch (2.5cm) brush

DÉCOUPAGE
4 sheets of wrapping paper depicting huge
   peonies, roses, or other blooms of your choice
Small sharp scissors
Craft knife
Wallpaper adhesive
Glue brush
Pasting boards

Small sponge or paper towels
Piece of white chalk

ANTIQUE GOLD
Tubes of gold and raw umber artists' acrylics
No. 5 artist's brush
Lidded container or jar
Water to mix • Paper towels

HAND-PAINTED DECORATION
Materials as for the antique gold, plus small tubes
   of Hooker's green, Payne's gray, and white
   artists' acrylics

VARNISHING
Tack cloth
Small can of satin polyurethane varnish or
   shellac
1 inch (2.5cm) brush
Fine-grade sandpaper
Mineral spirits

• preparation •

1   Screens are usually constructed either from fiberboard or particleboard, or from a wooden frame with plywood panels, and in each case will require sanding until smooth, working in the same direction as the grain. Plywood will require more preparation and paint, but the result will be worthwhile.

2   Apply a coat of white acrylic primer and leave to dry. Sand the whole thing again and you will be surprised at the improvement in the surface, although you may have to persevere with the panels. Apply two or three more coats until you are satisfied there is a good cover.

3   Apply two or three coats of the color you have chosen for the frame, and allow to dry. Lastly paint the pale color on the panels.

• antique gold •

Apply antique gold to the inside edge of each panel, as described on page 13. The gold can also be painted onto the outside edge of the screen. Keep a piece of damp paper towel at hand to whisk off any gold paint which accidentally strays onto the surface.

• découpage •

1   Cut a good selection of huge blooms, buds, and as many leaves as possible, choosing a variety of colors and

▶ *THE HUGE peonies decorating this screen are simple to cut.*

shapes. Lay the screen down flat onto a working-height surface. Arrange the cutout pieces into a design over the inside panels, remembering to reverse the flowers by cutting and reshaping them, or altering their angle, to give the panels a balanced "mirrored" look.

2 When you are happy with the design, hold it in place while marking around the edges of the paper with white chalk to indicate the cutouts' position when removed for pasting. Because the design is overlaid, remove the uppermost pieces and mark around those below.

3 Turn each cutout face down onto the pasting board and brush on the glue evenly, taking it out over the edges. Turn upright and place in position on the panel, working the excess glue and air from the middle outward with a rolling finger movement. When every blemish is removed and the cutout is flat, press the edges down. Continue in the same way until you are happy with the picture. **Stand back and look** occasionally; if it is possible to position the screen in an indirect light,

it will show up any air bubbles or little creases. Excess glue can be cleaned off as you work with dampened paper towels.

4 Leave the design to dry out thoroughly before using a small sponge or paper towel to clean both the background and surface of the paper.

5 It is a matter of personal taste whether you wish to decorate the outside panels in the same fashion, or with a small posy of flowers in one corner, each corner, or for the flowers to cascade from the top, as I have done. Follow the guidelines previously given.

• *finishing* •

If desired, brighten up the frame by hand-painting a twisted ribbon, bows, and leaves, as described on page 22. Leave to dry, then varnish as described on pages 13–14. Varnish the inner panels first (the frame can be given a couple of coats at the end), and brush the varnish in one direction (top to bottom).

PEONIES CASCADE from the top of the screen, and hand-painted ribbons and leaves add interest to the frame.

FIRE SCREEN

This fire screen turned out to be an absolutely stunning piece of work. The wonderful hollyhocks in full bloom positively glow against the dark background which shows them up in their full splendor. Smaller, darker flowers are scattered on the dark paint-finish; some actually merge into it, giving the whole picture dimension and depth. The fire screen measures 32 inches high × 23 inches wide (80 × 57cm) and is constructed from plywood in a pine frame, standing on two feet. Similar screens may be found at antiques stores. Ask a dealer to look out for one.

◆ *materials list* ◆

FIRE SCREEN

PREPARATION
Medium- and fine-grade sandpaper

PAINTING
Small can of white acrylic primer
Small can of black flat latex paint
1 inch (2.5cm) brush
Small natural sponge
Small cans of light- to mid-blue and raw
   umber flat latex paint **or** large tubes of
   artists' acrylics in the same colors
2 lidded containers
Polyvinyl white glue
Old spoon for measuring
Water to mix

DÉCOUPAGE
3 sheets of good-quality wrapping paper
Small sharp scissors

Craft knife
Wallpaper adhesive
Small glue brush
Pasting boards
Small sponge or paper towels
Piece of white chalk

ANTIQUE GOLD
Small tubes of gold and raw umber artists'
   acrylics
No. 4 artist's brush
Lidded container or jar
Water to mix

VARNISHING
Tack cloth
Small can of satin polyurethane varnish or
   shellac
1 inch (2.5cm) brush
Fine-grade sandpaper   ◆   Mineral spirits

◆ *preparation* ◆

1 Sand the whole screen down using medium-grade sandpaper, working in the same direction as the grain in the wood.

2 Apply a coat of white acrylic primer and when this is dry, sand the screen down again. Apply two more coats of white acrylic primer. When dry, sand all the surfaces with fine sandpaper until the finish feels smooth to the touch.

3 Apply two or three coats of black flat latex paint to both sides of the screen, including the frame, legs, and feet.

4 Measure out one tablespoon of blue latex paint and the same amount of white glue with up to four tablespoons of water. Mix the glaze. In a second container mix a small quantity of raw umber paint glaze, as above. Try to approach this project as if it were a painting or a work of art (which it is after all). There should be great depth in the background to enable flowers of a similar deep color to merge into it, while the huge pale blooms of the hollyhocks catch the light in the foreground.

5 Paint the top half of the board blue, the bottom half black, going over it until the color is strong. To avoid a straight line where the colors meet, use the tip of the brush to merge the colors while the paint is still wet. To soften the paint finish, a little raw umber can be sponged over the blue in patches to get some depth into the picture. Let the sponging go over onto the frame.

◆ *découpage* ◆

1 Lay the panel on a working-height surface with the legs sticking out in front. If you are able to get hold of this wonderful hollyhock paper (Huijsum Hollyhocks by National Gallery, No. 300133), you will see it has everything to offer in light and shade, and the background is similar in color to the screen. The huge white flowers have been reshaped, the tall center stem elongated, and another bud or two added to balance the overall picture. The pale green buds and leaves catch the light, and the flowers appear to grow from the base of the screen.

Cut out several large blooms and a lot of leaves. The selection is limited and you must improvise: by reshaping the same leaves and by using them at different angles they will appear more varied. The long central stem is elongated to twice its original length by cutting two stems and carefully overlaying one onto the other so that no seam is discernible. This stem and the largest blooms

were stuck down first and the remainder added around them. I hope you will enjoy doing it as much as I did.

2 When you have cut a good selection of flowers, buds, and leaves, lay the long central stem onto the panel and add the large blooms around the base. Check that it is centered and chalk around it, leaving the shape on the background. This will be a tremendous help when you have to remove the pieces for pasting. Add leaves and buds, building up the design; mark it out again.

3 Turn each cutout face down onto the pasting board and brush on the glue evenly over the surface, taking the brush out over the edges of the paper. A craft knife is useful to lift the cutouts off the board. Turn right side up and position on the screen. Press any excess glue and air bubbles out, working from the center of each bloom outward with a rolling finger movement, and wipe away with damp paper towels. When every blemish has been removed and the surface is flat, press down the edges. Try the flowers and leaves in their positions, building up the design and filling in gaps as you go along. Think whether they need to be overlaid or their stems tucked under a flower, and so on. **Stand back and look** occasionally. Last of all, add the dark blooms, placing them in different positions until you are happy with the design. Leave to dry.

4 Remove all traces of glue from the surface of the paper and the background using a damp sponge or paper towel. Leave to dry.

◆ *finishing* ◆

Apply an antique gold finish to the inside edge of the frame with the greatest care, as described on page 13. Have some dampened paper towels near you to whisk off any gold that accidentally strays onto the picture. Leave to dry, then varnish as described on pages 13–14. Apply the first coat of varnish sparingly – this is important, otherwise the white blooms will absorb the varnish and lose their vibrance and beauty. Apply sufficient layers to lose the edges of the paper and the "stuck on" look. The more you apply, the greater dimension and depth the picture will have. Stand back and admire.

▶ *HUGE HOLLYHOCKS glow against the dark background of this fire screen.*

THREE-FOLD SCREEN

The design on this lavishly decorated screen is applied to a strong red background, and uses a paper which is taken from a print of a French tapestry, circa 1490, entitled "The Lady and the Unicorn" and published by Caspari. The paper is very beautiful in its own right and it seems dreadful to dissect it in such a way, but the colors were perfect for the effect I was trying to achieve.

The magnificent heavenly angels which emerge from the background are taken from a Christmas giftwrap "Adoration of the Angels" published by Alan Hutchison Ltd. Parts of the design have been elaborately decorated with gilded scrolls and the "carved" frame is created from hand-colored photocopies of a Renaissance carving which has been richly gilded in liquid gold leaf. Extravagant cords and tassels from Laura Ashley add the finishing touch to this sumptuous project. The inner panels of the screen illustrated measure 62 inches × 17 inches (156 × 42cm). Visit antiques stores, you may find a similar screen languishing in a corner.

• materials list •

THREE-FOLD SCREEN
PREPARATION
Medium-grade sandpaper
Very fine-grade sandpaper
PAINTING
Can of white acrylic primer
Small can of tomato-red flat latex paint (or
  any color of your choice)
2 × 1 inch (2.5cm) brushes
DÉCOUPAGE
Up to 8 sheets of colorful background paper
  for the patchwork
6 sheets of "Adoration of the Angels" or a
  similar Christmas giftwrap
2 sheets of smaller angel paper, or any similar
  contrasting paper of your choice
Small sharp scissors
Craft knife
Wallpaper adhesive
Glue brush

At least two pasting boards, preferably more
Small sponge and paper towels
Container of water
Piece of white chalk
HAND-PAINTED DECORATION
Small can of dark- or mid-brown latex paint
Small bottle of liquid gold leaf (alcohol-based)
No. 5 artist's brush
VARNISHING
Tack cloth
Quart (2 liter) can of satin polyurethane varnish or
  pale shellac
1 inch (2.5cm) brush
Fine-grade sandpaper
Mineral spirits
OPTIONAL
If your screen is constructed of plywood, you
may need to mix a paint glaze and will therefore
need polyvinyl white glue and a lidded jar or
container.

• preparation •

Work on each panel separately and hinge them together when the work is completed.

If your screen is made from plywood, it is important to spend time on the preparation because plywood has a telltale straight "grain" and can have very rough, splintery patches. When painting or sanding down, *always* work in the same direction as the grain.

1 Use a sheet of medium-grade sandpaper to rub down the frame thoroughly. A coat of sanding sealer may be applied to a new frame and knots in softwood should be treated with a knotting sealer. *Do not sand the panels at this stage.*

2 Apply the first coat of white acrylic primer. Paint the frame, as well as the inner panels. Leave to dry. This will strengthen any loose splintery areas of plywood making sanding possible.

▶ *MAGNIFICENT ANGELS emerge from a lavish patchwork background of color – all cut from wrapping paper.*

3 Using medium-grade sandpaper, sand the whole thing down, again paying particular attention to the worst patches. If the patchiness and roughness can not be eradicated (which is quite usual), mix a glaze using equal parts of flat latex paint and white glue, mixed with up to four parts of water. Use the flat latex paint in the color you have chosen for the screen's topcoat.

4 Apply the glaze to the screen and frame, and allow to dry. Apply another two coats and you will find that the surface has improved dramatically.

If your screen is made from medium-density fiberboard or particleboard

1 Apply the first coat of white acrylic primer and leave to dry.

2 Use a sheet of medium sandpaper and sand down the whole thing until it feels smooth to the touch, especially the edges. Remember when sanding to always sand in one direction only.

3 Dust off and apply another three coats of acrylic primer, allowing it to dry between coats and sanding down any build-up of paint on the edges as you go along, using the fine sandpaper.

4 Apply two or three coats of the color you have chosen for the screen's topcoat.

• *the frame* •

Paint and decorate the frame first, then there will be no likelihood of splashing paint onto your découpage design.

1 The simplest method is to paint the frame a brown wood color and, when it is dry, to paint bold scrolls and squiggles to represent the carving.

2 An alternative is to use photocopies of wood carving printed on sheets of paper. Photocopies of wood carvings and ornamental scrolls are available from Dover Inc. (see suppliers list on page 142) in a book entitled *Ornamental Borders, Scrolls and Cartouches*. (Yet another option is to stain the frame in a wood color of your choice, or to paint it in antique gold – see page 13.) Begin by painting all the sheets of paper with watered-down brown latex paint – the paint you used for the frame will do – which will allow the detail to show through. Allow to dry out. Then cut out the painted carvings, paste the back of each strip individually, and apply to the frame, butting the edges of the next strip to it. Stick the photocopies on all three panels and allow to dry out.

Color in the carving using the brown paint in normal strength, omitting the uppermost pieces which you will highlight next with liquid gold leaf. Allow to dry, then with an artist's brush highlight the remaining carving with liquid gold leaf. **Stand back occasionally** to observe your work from a distance. Paint around the inside edge of the frame and don't worry if you stray a little onto the panel – it will be covered later by the découpage design.

3 Paint the outside edge of the frame in antique gold acrylics, see page 13. Allow the whole thing to dry.

• *découpage* •

You will find it much easier to work if the panel is laid on a flat surface, such as a tabletop. Alternatively, the three sections can be placed against a wall or on the floor, but the latter may cause you some discomfort because you will have to kneel down for long periods.

1 Begin by cutting the colorful background paper into different shapes, dissecting the different colors separately. Make up your own patchwork for the background; concentrate on cutting a good number of shapes in as wide a variety as possible. The patterns can be used in any direction to provide more interest, but any animals look decidedly better on their feet.

The paper cutouts have to be juggled about like a jigsaw puzzle to fill in the gaps. Cut triangles, squares, rectangles, and ovals, in fact any shape at all, to utilize every tiny piece of pattern and color on a sheet.

2 **First outside panel** Begin by laying the pieces of cutout paper on the top of the first panel, fitting them into the upper corners. At the same time, cut out the first row of angels, selecting the three on the top row of the screen. Lay them down on the panel to see whether they fit into the space, or if they need to be trimmed. The patchwork should completely surround the angels, being large enough to fit slightly underneath them. If it is helpful, chalk around the shapes in position, marking their outline onto the colored panel; otherwise, fit them in as you go along.

Turn each cutout face down onto the pasting board and brush the glue evenly over the surface, taking the brush out over the edges of the paper. A craft knife is useful to lift the cutouts from the board. Turn right side up and position on the panel, pressing out any excess glue and air bubbles, and wiping away glue with damp paper towels.

3 Fit the angels into position again. If they cover the background of patchwork, chalk around them. If not, paste on more background shapes to fill any gaps. Paste angels and place within the chalk marks. Press down from the middle outward, leaving the edges loose until all the air and glue has been worked out to the edges. Then press the edges down.

The top of the panel to the bottom of the first block of angels (two rows) measures 21 inches (53cm) – see below. Cut out and paste another section of patchwork about 8½ inches (21cm) deep before the next block of angels. Repeat the same procedure each time.

4   If you are using the same paper as I have, alterations will have to be made to the last row of angels because they are too wide to fit the panel. Do try to dissect and reshape them logically; this is not nearly as complicated as it sounds, since the cutting is simple and straight-forward. The main thing is always to lay the paper shapes onto the panel to see what they look like and how they fit, and make the necessary alterations before continuing.

5   **Second outside panel** Repeat steps 2 to 4. It is vital that the two outer panels should be the same. Now is the time to stand them upright beside one another to either measure or mark out the design. The height at which the rows of angels start must coincide, because their halos are very noticeable.

6   **Middle panel** Repeat steps 2 to 4. I have used a different paper with a smaller motif, introducing the larger angels at the base to tie the overall design together.

◆ *scroll work (optional)* ◆

Paint sheets of scrolls with watered-down, brown flat latex paint (as you did with the "carving" for the frame). Allow the paint to dry out thoroughly. Paste and apply to the panels wherever you think best, especially if there are ugly edges within the découpage that would benefit from being covered over!

Allow all three panels to dry out thoroughly. Clean the surfaces carefully with a damp sponge or paper towels.

◆ *varnishing* ◆

Place all three panels in an upright position. Clean off any dust from the frames and panels with a tack cloth. Apply the first coat of varnish sparingly and allow to dry.

Apply approximately 10 coats of varnish to the inside panels, cleaning each with a tack cloth and allowing to dry thoroughly between each coat. The frames will require about four coats of varnish. When the panels are quite dry, attach the hinges. You will have an exceptionally sturdy piece of furniture and one which, I am sure, will look absolutely superb.

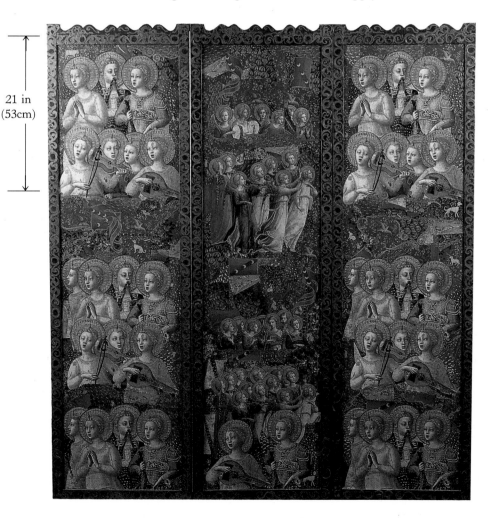

21 in (53cm)

THE HEIGHT at which the rows of angels start on the outside panels should coincide because their halos are very noticeable.

8

THE BEDROOM

Che character of our bedroom may change over the years, but it should always be a sanctuary, a very personal and private place – not always possible if there are small children in the house! It should have a romantic feel, be functional, yet cozy in the colder months, comfortable and quiet for rest and sleep, and fresh and airy when the windows are flung wide in fine weather to allow sunlight, breeze, and birdsong to filter in.

Make a rose découpage wreath for your bedside table, pretty up your vanity with a pair of candlestick lamps or a fabulous vanity set, or for a really romantic touch try decorating an enchanting floral headboard.

◆ ◆ ◆ ◆

FLORAL HEADBOARD

This headboard is made from medium-density fiberboard, but you can use particleboard of the best quality. Scour flea markets for unusually shaped designs. This can be a great way to freshen an old bedroom.

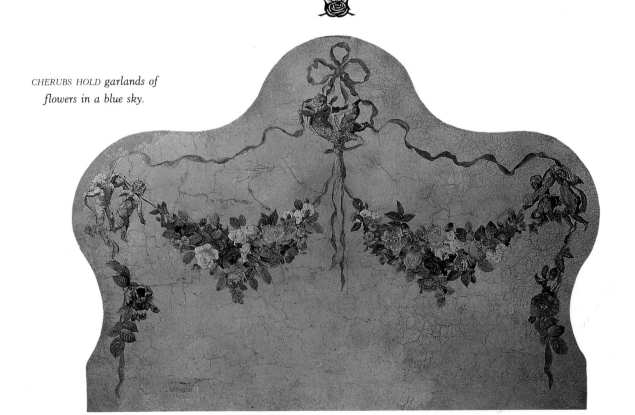

CHERUBS HOLD *garlands of flowers in a blue sky.*

◆

◆

• *materials list* •

HEADBOARD

PREPARATION

Medium- and fine-grade sandpaper

PAINTING

Small can of white acrylic primer

1 inch (2.5cm) brush

Small cans of mid-blue and pale turquoise blue
  latex paint

Small amount of yellow acrylic or latex paint to
  add sunlight (optional)

White primer used previously

Polyvinyl white glue

Lidded container

Natural sponge　　　◆　　　Water to mix

DÉCOUPAGE

6 sheets of good-quality wrapping paper (these
  can be mixed as long as they are of the same
  thickness) illustrated with roses

A sheet of paper with cherubs

Small sharp scissors　◆　Craft knife

Wallpaper adhesive

Glue brush　◆　Pasting boards

Small sponge or paper towels

Piece of white chalk

ANTIQUE GOLD

Tubes of gold and raw umber artists' acrylics

No. 4 artist's brush

Lidded container or jar

Water to mix

CRAQUELURE

Materials as listed on page 25

• *preparation* •

1 Rub down the edges of the headboard with medium-grade sandpaper. Remove dust; paint both sides of the headboard with white acrylic primer. Leave to dry. Rub down the edges with fine-grade sandpaper. Feel it with your fingers to make sure it is smooth. Apply two more coats of primer, letting it dry between coats.

2 Paint on two coats of mid-blue latex paint to both sides, and allow to dry. For the "right" side mix the paint glaze by combining one tablespoon of pale turquoise blue, one tablespoon of white glue, and approximately three tablespoons of water. The aim is to produce a sky-like effect (see page 19 for sponging techniques). Sponge on the pale turquoise color in

places. Dip the sponge as it is into the darker color and sponge on in patches. Sponge on white, especially at the top of the headboard. Leave to dry for a while before softly sponging on some more white for cottony clouds. Leave to dry.

• *découpage* •

1 Make two or three chalk marks at different points to indicate the center of the headboard. Chalk a floppy bow at the top. Mark the positions of the three groups of cherubs on the headboard; cut them out and paste on first. Draw the ribbons and outline the swags in chalk (they can be erased several times until you get them right). See pages 22–5 for hand-painted finishing touches.

2 Cut a good selection of roses and leaves, and place them on the headboard to form an attractive design. When you are satisfied with it, chalk around the outline.

3 Place the cutouts face down on the pasting board and brush the glue evenly over the surface, making sure the edges are covered. Turn right side up with a craft knife, if it is helpful, and position on the headboard. Work out any air bubbles, blemishes, and excess glue with your fingers, wiping it away carefully with damp paper towels. This is an overlaid design that can be built up gradually, sticking on a few of the choicest blooms in the uppermost positions, particularly those which will catch the light. Leaves are very important to add depth to the work and for a natural look.

When the cutouts are flat, press the edges of each one down as you proceed. When the decoration is finished, leave it to dry. **Stand back and look,** and if any gaps require filling in, do so now. When the surface is dry, the work can be cleaned up with a damp sponge or paper towel. Leave to dry.

• *hand-painted decoration* •

Paint the gold ribbons and bow as described on page 22 using antique gold (see page 13). Shade the ribbons well using raw umber on the same brush as the gold, painting the ribbon to join up with the découpage swags to complete the picture. Leave to dry.

• *finishing* •

Apply a single coat of satin varnish to protect the découpage. Leave to dry, then apply an antique craquelure finish (see page 26), followed by two coats of satin varnish. When the headboard is completely dry, polish with white beeswax polish as described on page 83.

◆

CANDLESTICK LAMPS

*Here is something really special for your bedroom. Take time to think about a design and color that will
complement your décor. Use tiny forget-me-nots or rosebuds, blossoms, or tiny hummingbirds with miniature
pink cherry blossoms for an oriental feel; twist and twine leaves and flowers down the stem with a hand-painted
ribbon, and gild the moldings as a finishing touch.*
*The candlesticks can be sponge-finished first in a delicate shade (see page 19), or simply painted in latex paint.
Most fine lighting stores carry faux candles, brass holders, electrified or liquid candles, and the candlesticks
themselves. The shades are also available – why not découpage the shade, too?*

◆

◆ *materials list* ◆

PAIR OF WOODEN CANDLESTICKS
  approximately 8–10 inches (20–25cm) high
PREPARATION
Very fine-grade sandpaper
PAINTING
Small can of white acrylic primer
Small brush
Small can of cream (or color of your choice)
  flat or semigloss latex paint
DÉCOUPAGE
Good-quality wrapping paper illustrated with
  tiny rosebuds or other delicate motifs
Small sharp scissors
Craft knife
Wallpaper paste
Glue brush
Pasting board
Small sponge or paper towels
ANTIQUE GOLD
Small tubes of gold and raw umber artists'
  acrylics
No. 4 artist's brush
Lidded container or jar
Water to mix
VARNISHING
Tack cloth
Small can of satin polyurethane varnish or
  shellac
Small brush
Fine-grade sandpaper
Mineral spirits
ACCESSORIES
2 brass holders and 2 candleshades of your
  choice

◆ *preparation* ◆

1 If necessary, rub down the candlesticks with sandpaper, checking the rim and base edges are smooth.
2 Apply at least two coats of white acrylic primer, allowing it to dry between coats.
3 Apply two coats of cream latex paint, turning the candlestick upside down to check that all the surface is covered. Leave to dry.

◆ *découpage* ◆

The candlesticks can be decorated in a number of ways; have a look at porcelain candlesticks in antiques stores to get some good ideas. Tiny rosebuds, birds, ribbons, trailing ivy leaves, or honeysuckle can look lovely on the stem with a few larger blooms on the base. The choice is yours.
1 Cut out with great care because intricate flowers and stems will look unattractive with the background showing. If the stems are long, fine, and curling, cut them into sections and butt them together when they are pasted and applied to the surface. The seams will not show if they are done accurately.
2 Turn each paper cutout face down onto the pasting board and apply the glue evenly over the surface, taking it out over the edges onto the board to make sure that the edges have glue on them. Lift from the board using a craft knife, turn right side up, and paste to the candlestick. Press out excess glue and air bubbles with your fingers, wiping it away with a damp paper towel. When the surface of the paper is flat, press down the edges.
3 When the decoration is complete, leave to dry before cleaning up the surface of the paper and background with a damp sponge or paper towel.

◆ *finishing* ◆

Apply an antique gold finish to the moldings, working as described on page 13. Allow to dry, then varnish as described on pages 13–14, taking care that the varnish doesn't gather and run on the moldings. Five coats will probably suffice.

◀ *CANDLESHADES and candles echo the deep pink of the*
rosebuds on the candlesticks.

VANITY SET

In most homes it is not uncommon to find one or two old items which have become scratched, faded, or worn. These may be tin, enamel, plastic, or wood. The oval tin tray fell into this category, and was perfect for transformation. The hand mirror was discolored white plastic which looked most unattractive, but nevertheless had a pleasing shape. An old hairbrush of a similar shape could, perhaps, be found to complete the set.

◆ materials list ◆

METAL TRAY AND PLASTIC MIRROR
PREPARATION
Red oxide primer
Small can of flat varnish (or small can of shellac,
    thinned with denatured alcohol)
2 × 1 inch (2.5cm) brushes
Mineral spirits
Paper towels
PAINTING
White acrylic primer
Small cans of cream and white semigloss latex
    paint
Small brush
Lidded container or jar
Small natural sponge
Water to mix
DÉCOUPAGE
Paper covered in the tiniest roses and other
    pretty flowers, buds, and leaves
Small sharp scissors
Craft knife
Wallpaper paste
Glue brush   ◆   Pasting board
Small sponge or paper towels
Piece of white chalk
ANTIQUE GOLD
Small tubes of gold and raw umber artists'
    acrylics
No. 4 artist's brush
Lidded container or jar
Water to mix
VARNISHING
Tack cloth
Small can of satin polyurethane varnish or
    shellac
1 inch (2.5cm) brush

◆ decorating the tray ◆

1 Prepare the tray as described on pages 15–18. When the red oxide primer is completely dry, apply white acrylic primer followed by two or three coats of white semigloss latex paint.

2 Apply a simple sponged-on paint finish (see page

◀ *A* PLASTIC *mirror and tin tray completely transformed: this delightful pair would grace any vanity.*

19), using cream semigloss latex lightly sponged over the surface at random. Dip the tip of the sponge directly into the can and keep sponging all over the surface until it looks even, but with the white still visible.

3 Chalk a vague diamond shape onto the surface of the tray, and stick on one or two flowers to mark out the shape. From this rough guide, the rest of the flowers and leaves are stuck on like a jigsaw puzzle – wherever their shape looks as if it will fit. Many of the flowers shown are overlapped by others, and leaves and buds have been tucked into gaps.

Place each cutout face down onto the pasting board and apply the paste, making sure that the edges are covered. Lift with a craft knife and position on the tray. This is called an overlaid design. Although quite time-consuming, it is relatively easy because there is no set pattern or design; the flowers and leaves are pasted down in every direction, but it is useful to keep turning the tray around to check that the shape looks balanced from all angles. If the overall shape is slightly off-center, the hand-painted ribbons (see below) will even the whole thing out.

4 When completely dry, clean the work to remove excess glue from the surface using damp paper towels or a small sponge.

5 Apply an antique gold finish to the outside rim of the tray, as described on page 13. Then add some twisted ribbons and bows, or other decoration of your choice, using the techniques described on pages 22–5. Finally, varnish as described on pages 13–14.

◆ decorating the hand mirror ◆

1 Paint the mirror back and frame with two coats of flat varnish or shellac, allowing it to dry between coats. Apply two coats of white primer, again allowing to dry, followed by two coats of white semigloss latex. Be careful not to smudge paint onto the mirror glass.

2 Apply a cream sponge finish, as before.

3 Use the leftover paper from the tray to decorate the hand mirror. There is no need to chalk a shape this time; simply follow the shape of the mirror, pasting on the flowers facing in different directions. Start from the middle, so the flowers around the outside show up clearly above the others, giving the design depth. Allow to dry.

4 After cleaning the excess glue from the surface of the work, paint a bow and a broken ribbon through the flowers, ending with two trailing ribbons on the handle. Allow to dry, then varnish as before.

9
THE GUEST ROOM

*P*retty bed linen, scented herb sachets for the drawers, fresh flowers, magazines and books, fresh fruit, and gold-wrapped chocolates all help to provide a welcome when friends are coming to stay.

Smarten up an old bureau with a paint finish, or découpage a mirror or picture frame. Perhaps you have a lovely big tray to decorate, on which your guests could enjoy early morning coffee or breakfast in bed.

♦ ♦ ♦ ♦

OCTAGONAL MIRROR

I bought this old frame for next to nothing. As you can see from the photograph, it has been transformed by painting it a gorgeous shade of turquoise blue with a simple design of single hand-painted roses taken from an eighteenth-century textile print. The roses are "tied" together with a twisted ribbon painted in acrylics.

◆ *materials list* ◆

MIRROR FRAME
PREPARATION
Small can of flat varnish (or shellac thinned
   with denatured alcohol)
1 inch (2.5cm) brush
PAINTING
Small can of white acrylic primer
Small can of turquoise latex paint
Small brush
DÉCOUPAGE
Wrapping paper with a rose design
Small sharp scissors
Craft knife
Wallpaper adhesive
Small glue brush

Pasting board ◆ Small sponge or paper towels
ANTIQUE GOLD
Tubes of gold and raw umber artists' acrylics
No. 4 artist's brush
Lidded container or jar
Water to mix
VARNISHING
Tack cloth
Small can of satin polyurethane varnish or
   shellac
1 inch (2.5cm) brush
Mineral spirits
Mirror glass can be ordered and cut to your
requirements at some hardware stores, decorating
stores, and building-supply stores

◆ *preparation* ◆

1   Paint the frame with two coats of flat varnish or shellac to seal it and stop the dark stain seeping into the paint. Let it dry between coats.
2   Apply two coats of white primer and let it dry. Then apply at least two coats of the turquoise latex paint. Allow to dry.

◆ *découpage* ◆

1   This is a simple design using only the rose blooms. Cut out as many as you need.
2   Turn each cutout face down on the pasting board and

apply the glue evenly all over. Turn right side up using a craft knife and apply to the frame, working the air and glue out with your fingers until the surface is flat. Then press down the edges. Let it dry.
3   When the work is completely dry, clean up the surface with a damp sponge or paper towel.

◆ *finishing* ◆

Decorate in antique gold (page 13), painting ribbons and bows, as described on pages 22–5. Leave to dry, then varnish as described on pages 13–14.

◄ ROSES AND RIBBONS *adorn an octagonal mirror.*

PARCHMENT BUREAU

A Victorian pine bureau of inferior quality, "grained" to cover its shortcomings, and probably built originally for servants' quarters, has been transformed by a charming parchment finish, hand-painted with swags of leaves and berries, and aged and craquelured.
The paint finish is all applied with a sponge. The swags of leaves and berries are hand-painted and easy to master after a little initial practice on paper. Even without decoration, the bureau would be attractive in this lovely ocher color which works well with most color schemes.

◆ *materials list* ◆

WOODEN BUREAU
PREPARATION
Medium-grade sandpaper
Very fine-grade sandpaper
If your furniture has been stained in a dark color
    you will also need a small can of flat varnish
    (or shellac thinned with denatured alcohol) and
    an old brush
PAINTING
Small can of white acrylic primer
Small can of gardenia or other pale cream
    semigloss latex paint
Small tubes of yellow ocher, white, raw
    umber, or Payne's gray artists' acrylics

1 inch (2.5cm) brush
Polyvinyl white glue
Lidded container or carton
Small natural sponge
Water to mix
HAND-PAINTED DECORATION
Small tubes of Hooker's green and Venetian
    red artists' acrylics
Payne's gray and white, as above
No. 4 artist's brush
A piece of white chalk
Paper towels
CRAQUELURE
Materials as listed on page 25

► *A PRETTY BUREAU, which would fit into almost any color scheme.*

◆ *preparation – painted item* ◆

Remove the handles and the drawers from the frame. With medium-grade sandpaper, rub down the bureau, and drawers, always working in the same direction as the grain in the wood, if you can see it.

Sand through the paint on the edges of drawers, top, locks, and escutcheons. This will provide a "key" on which to paint.

(*NOTE*   If the bureau has many layers of paint that have become uneven, blistered, or unsightly, it may be better to use the services of a professional furniture-stripping company, who often collect and deliver. If you have a lot of time and patience, you can use a proprietary paint stripper.)

◆ *preparation – dark-stained wood* ◆

If the bureau is stained, it will discolor the paint. To avoid this, a barrier has to be formed between the two. Rub down, as above, with medium-grade sandpaper, remove dust, and paint the bureau with either a coat of flat varnish or two coats of shellac thinned a little with denatured alcohol (allow shellac 30 minutes between coats). Let it dry.

◆ *painting* ◆

1 Apply a coat of white acrylic primer and let it dry. Run your fingers over the frame and the drawers, and smooth out any rough patches with very fine-grade sandpaper. Apply at least another two coats of

DETAIL OF *a craquelure finish.*

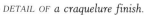

CHALK THE OUTLINE of your chosen shape onto the top of the chest. Paint the stem and leaves, returning to shade them, and filling in with berries to balance the design.

acrylic primer, allowing it to dry between coats. Check drawer edges for any build-up of paint that may affect their closing and remove with sandpaper, if necessary.

2 Apply two coats of semigloss latex paint in gardenia or another pale cream color and let it dry.

3 Mix a paint glaze using equal parts of white latex paint and white glue (two tablespoons of each will be enough), mixed with 1–4 parts water. Using the container's lid as a palette, squeeze out about an inch of yellow ocher tube paint, a spoonful of pale cream, and a tiny blob of raw umber or Payne's gray. These will have to be replenished as you go along. Have a spoonful of white paint on the lid if there is room.

4 Apply the sponged paint-finish. Start with the sides to get the hang of it before tackling the front. Replace the drawers so the paint finish can cover the whole surface and the lines can flow. Ease the drawers out a little using a screwdriver in their keyholes when you have finished, to avoid the drawers sticking. Squeeze the sponge out in water, removing any excess on paper towels. Dip a little of the sponge in the glaze, then into the yellow ocher. Work from a top corner sponging diagonally; dip the sponge into two colors at once, and cover the surface with some basic markings to give it movement and shape, filling in other areas with a paler color. The desired effect is illustrated on page 20.

5 Leave to dry before building up the paint further. Anything you dislike can be whited out and altered. Introduce a thin vein of Payne's gray or patches of raw umber to add depth and interest. Wash the sponge several times while you are working, when it becomes impossible to differentiate between the colors. It is a matter of choice whether the color is vibrant or delicate; colors can be intensified, but the overall effect of a subdued parchment finish is a lovely glow of soft yellow, and you will find that it fits into many different room schemes.

◆ *hand-painted leaves and berries* ◆

Using the keyhole as a guide, make a vertical chalk mark in the center of each drawer and an inch (2.5cm) in from either edge; join together with a deep curve. This may take several attempts – wipe away mistakes until all the curves look the same. Decorate using the techniques described on pages 22–3.

◆ *finishing* ◆

Apply an antique craquelure finish (see page 26), and polish as described on page 83.

ROSE WREATH TABLE

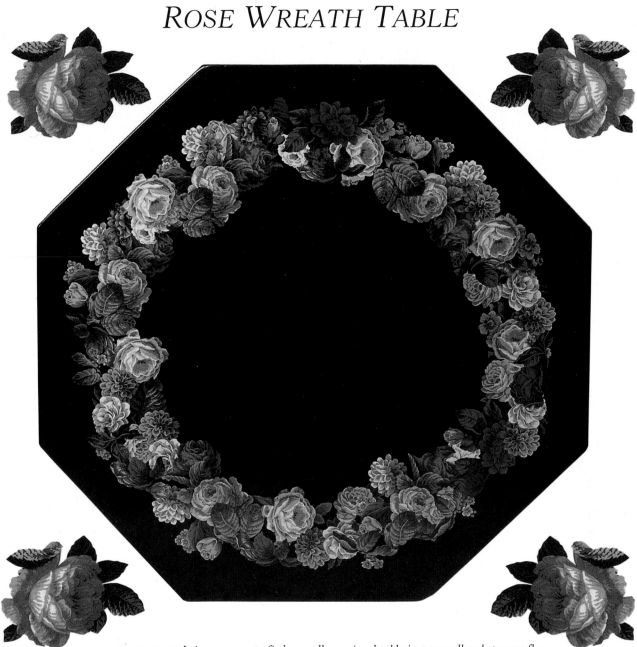

ROSE WREATH TABLE *It is very easy to find a small occasional table in a secondhand store or flea market; you may even have one in your home which can be transformed. This old mahogany table was first stripped and then painted with several coats of black flat latex paint. It is a good idea to turn the table upside down onto a working-height surface to apply the first coat of paint; when it is dry, turn the table upright and paint everywhere else. Leave to dry and apply further coats until you are satisfied with the coverage.*

The découpage design was easily cut from a sheet of good-quality wrapping paper covered in roses. Since the tabletop is octagonal, a wreath of flowers arranged in a rough circle looks rather pretty with a central posy on the tray base. The table was very dented and uneven, but the surface has been greatly improved by the application of many layers of varnish. The entire project cost very little, and the result is a most attractive bedside table. Polish occasionally with clear wax polish to give it a lovely patina and depth.

BREAKFAST TRAY

LARGE BREAKFAST TRAY Perfect for treating your guests to breakfast in bed the next time they visit. Paint-finished with the leftovers from the parchment bureau, and decorated in a wonderful paper illustrating antique roses, lilies, and morning glories, which was used on the Edwardian jug and fat coffeepot (pages 38 and 32), and, with other papers, on the commode (page 69).

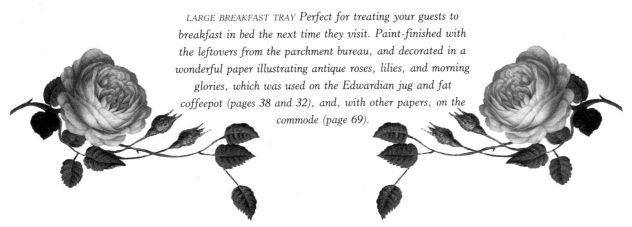

♦

10
THE BATHROOM AND DRESSING ROOM

*B*athrooms can be so boring. Those in modern houses often have little or no natural light and are tiled from floor to ceiling, making them practical, but sterile, places. A piece of furniture can transform a bathroom. A small chest, cupboard, vanity, or washstand is very well suited to this room; add a few pictures on the walls and some fresh flowers to bring life and comfort to an otherwise dull and purely functional area. The projects shown would adorn a dressing room equally effectively.

◆　◆　◆　◆

A BLUE SPONGED finish on a white background has brought this shabby washstand to life.

VICTORIAN WASHSTAND

Simple sponging and delicately colored flowers, cut from wrapping paper and formed into bunches, have transformed a shabby washstand into a charming piece of furniture, which would make an eye-catching focal point in a bathroom or dressing room.
When I stripped the paint from this (probably homemade) washstand I found burn marks, immovable black ink stains on the top surface, and an unsightly jumble of ill-matched wood. One of the back legs had been replaced due to woodworm.
The washstand shown measures 29 × 24 × 16 inches (72 × 60 × 39cm). It has been painted with white semigloss latex paint, and simply and quickly sponged with a blue, transparent fast-drying paint glaze before applying the découpage decoration.
The pretty little jug, bowl, mug, and chamberpot were collected from different sources over a period of time and made into a set using matching decoration.

◆ *materials list* ◆

WASHSTAND
PREPARATION
Medium-grade sandpaper
Small can of flat varnish or shellac thinned
    with denatured alcohol (if your furniture has
    been stained a dark color)
1 inch (2.5cm) brush
PAINTING
Small can of white acrylic primer
Small can of white semigloss latex paint
Small can of pale to mid-blue latex paint
Polyvinyl white glue
1 inch (2.5cm) brush
Natural sponge
Old spoon for measuring
Lidded container or jar
Water to mix
DÉCOUPAGE
3 sheets of pretty wrapping paper, preferably
    illustrated with stemmed flowers
Small sharp scissors
Craft knife   ◆   Wallpaper paste
Glue brush   ◆   Pasting board
Small sponge or paper towels
VARNISHING
Tack cloth
Small can of satin polyurethane varnish or
    shellac
1 inch (2.5cm) brush
Mineral spirits

◆ *preparation* ◆

1a   If your washstand is already painted, rub it down thoroughly with medium-grade sandpaper to provide a "key" on which to paint.
1b   If it is stained a dark color, paint it with flat varnish or shellac to seal it and prevent the stain marking the paint. Let it dry.
1c   For a stripped pine washstand, as this one was, sand with medium-grade sandpaper in the direction of the wood grain, paying particular attention to edges.
2   Remove all dust. Apply the first coat of white primer and let it dry. Rub down again. Apply at least two more undercoats, allowing the paint to dry between each coat. Then apply two coats of white semigloss latex paint, again allowing to dry between coats.
3   Mix a transparent paint glaze of two tablespoons of blue paint, the same of white glue, and one to four tablespoons of water.
    Rinse sponge in cold water and remove excess moisture on paper towels. Dip the sponge into the paint glaze and squeeze it out. Using a light wrist movement, sponge the glaze all over the washstand. It is fast drying and the sponge will need replenishing frequently. Leave areas you plan to decorate lighter. Let it dry.

◆ *découpage* ◆

1   Cut out a good selection of flowers, stems, and leaves – the stems need not necessarily belong to the flowers: they can be arranged to look as if they do. It is helpful to arrange the design on a plain surface beside you until you are happy with it. The design in the photograph is overlaid, and the ribbon "tied around" the stems to look

◆

like a bunch of flowers is actually to hide the seams.

2   Turn each cutout face down on the pasting board and brush the glue evenly all over. The craft knife will be useful to lift them right side up again and to position the pieces on the washstand. Paste the underneath cutouts first, and build up the decoration until it is balanced and lifelike. Press out the excess glue and air bubbles with your fingers, wipe glue off with paper towels, and when

the cutouts are flat, press the edges down.

3   When the decoration is complete, leave it to dry. Then clean up the surface of the work with a damp sponge or paper towel.

◆ *finishing* ◆

Apply varnish as described on pages 13–14.

JUG, BOWL, CHAMBERPOT, AND MUG These tinware items make ideal accessories for your washstand. Prepare them all as described on pages 15–18. When the red oxide is dry, apply at least two coats of white acrylic primer, letting it dry between coats. For the top coat, apply two coats of white semigloss latex paint, letting it dry between coats. Sponge in exactly the same way as the washstand using the remaining glaze.

The insides of the accessories may be painted in plain blue or white. Decorate with delicate sprigs, using the same paper as the washstand. Apply an antique gold finish to rims and handles, as described on page 13. Let it dry, then varnish as before.

◆

11

THE MODERN NURSERY

*J*n today's smaller homes space is at a premium, and few children are fortunate enough to have a separate nursery or playroom. Many have their own bedroom, though, and the designs in this chapter will help to create a pretty and functional room in which children can spend their earliest years.

• • • •

TOY BOX WITH CLOWN DECORATION

Storage space for toys is essential to any nursery. An old bathroom laundry box, bought very cheaply, has been painted in bright colors and decorated in a simple, well-spaced design using birthday wrapping paper. I could not resist the clowns on this pretty turquoise background and decided to paint the box the same color. Luckily I found exactly the same shade in a ready-mixed paint.

• materials list •

LARGE BOX WITH LID	Small sharp scissors
PREPARATION	Craft knife
Medium-grade sandpaper	Wallpaper paste
PAINTING	Glue brush • Pasting board
Small can of white acrylic primer	Small sponge or paper towels
2 small cans of latex paint in colors of your	**VARNISHING**
choice, one for the outside and a contrast for	Tack cloth
inside	Small can of satin polyurethane varnish or
1 inch (2.5cm) brush	shellac
DÉCOUPAGE	1 inch (2.5cm) brush
3 sheets of paper with a clown motif	Fine-grade sandpaper
1 sheet of paper for cutting into borders	Mineral spirits

▶ *CUT A DESIGN from birthday wrapping paper to decorate the nursery or children's playroom.*

•

TOY BOX *with clown decoration. This bright, cheerful piece is ideal for any nursery or playroom.*

◆ *preparation* ◆

1   Sand down the old painted surface to form a "key" on which to paint.

2   Remove dust and apply two or three coats of white primer, allowing it to dry between coats. Prop the lid up to avoid sticking while the paint dries. Also paint the inside of the box.

3   Apply two or three coats of a top color to match your

décor, letting it dry between coats. When the inside undercoat is dry, paint on the contrasting color. Leave the lid open and allow to dry.

◆ *découpage* ◆

As you can see in the photograph, it was impossible to eliminate many of the ''HAPPY BIRTHDAY'' letters, but it doesn't seem to detract from the overall decoration.

1 Cut the borders first and stick them on, making the necessary adjustments at the corners to prevent creasing. Cut a large selection of clowns and a lot of extra balloons, and little motifs to fill in. Aim to decorate the box on all sides and on the top, as well as inside the lid.

2 Turn each cutout face down onto the pasting board and brush the paste evenly over the surface, making sure the edges are covered. Turn the cutouts right side up and stick onto the surface, gently pressing out excess glue and air bubbles with a rolling finger movement and working from the center outward. Wipe away glue with damp paper towels. You will find the craft knife useful for lifting the more delicate pieces from the pasting board and altering their position on the surface of the box. When you are satisfied that each cutout is flat, press down the edges. Continue in this way until the box is decorated, remembering to stand back and take a good look occasionally.

3 Leave the work to dry before cleaning up the surface with a damp sponge or paper towel.

◆ *finishing* ◆

Varnish the box as described on pages 13–14.

ROCKING-HORSE STOOL
Rocking horses brighten up an old stool, which was prepared and painted in the same way as the toy box. It is decorated with rocking horses cut from the border-type paper with colorful strips on the legs.

♦

DINOSAUR TRUNK

After the hype of Jurassic Park and the expensive merchandise it created, here is a unique (and cheap)
alternative. Children will appreciate the lovable dinosaurs which decorate their brightly painted tin trunk, and
it will be particularly special to them because you will have made it.
Old traveling trunks are easily found, but it is most important to be sure that when the lid is up, it stays up,
and will not fall shut on small fingers. There must be a prop on one side of the lid inside the trunk which locks
straight once the lid is up and has to be physically bent again before the lid will close. Choose a vibrant, fun
color and a contrasting one for the trimmings – any child will love it!

THIS TRUNK *provides* Jurassic Park *style as a low-budget feature.*

♦

◆ *materials list* ◆

LARGE BOX WITH HINGED LID AND SAFETY PROP

PREPARATION

If your trunk is metal: small can of red oxide
  metal primer

1 inch (2.5cm) brush

Mineral spirits

If your trunk is wooden: medium-grade sandpaper

PAINTING

Small can of white acrylic primer

2 small cans of bright color flat or semigloss latex
  paint (one for inside, one for outside)

Small can of vibrant contrasting flat or semigloss
  latex paint for trimmings

1 inch (2.5cm) brush

No. 8 artist's brush

DÉCOUPAGE

3 sheets of good-quality wrapping paper or
  birthday paper

Small sharp scissors

Craft knife

Wallpaper paste

Glue brush ◆ Pasting board

Small sponge or paper towels

VARNISHING

Tack cloth

Small can of satin polyurethane varnish or
  shellac

1 inch (2.5cm) brush

Mineral spirits

◆ *preparation* ◆

1 If your trunk is metal, prepare as described on pages 15–18. If wooden, sand with medium-grade sandpaper to provide a "key" for the paintwork.

2 Lift the trunk up onto a working-height surface. Apply two or three coats of white acrylic primer until the surface looks perfect. Allow paint to dry between coats. Paint on two or three coats of the top color – walk around it to check that every nook and cranny has been painted. When it is dry, remember to turn it upside down to paint underneath.

3 Paint the inside last, taking care with the top edge (when the lid is shut the contrasting inside color should not be visible). Leave the lid open and allow to dry.

◆ *découpage* ◆

1 Cut out a good selection of dinosaurs, balloons, and other little motifs to fill in.

2 Turn each cutout face down onto the pasting board and apply the glue, brushing it evenly over the surface and making sure the edges are covered. Use a craft knife to turn the cutouts right side up and place onto the surface of the trunk. Press out the excess glue and air bubbles with a rolling movement of the fingers until it is flat, before pressing down the edges. Wipe off excess glue with damp paper towels. Stand back and look at the design occasionally to appreciate it overall.

3 When the decoration is finished, leave it to dry out before cleaning up the surface with dampened paper towels.

◆ *finishing* ◆

With very slightly thinned paint, and using the No. 8 artist's brush, paint around all the trimmings, giving them three or four coats until the color is dense. Prop the lid up a little to avoid sticking. Allow to dry; then varnish as described on pages 13–14.

12
THE CONSERVATORY

*O*ld enamelware is ideal for a conservatory or sunroom, being both functional and decorative – perfect for displaying flowers and plants, useful for carrying water and for extra storage.

A collection of Victorian and Edwardian tinware, painted in dark country green, sits comfortably on an old garden table at the edge of the woods outside my house. The two exceptions are the traveling trunk, which is black and decorated with huge pink peonies and white blossoms, and the old pail, which is painted in buttermilk and applied with a simple design of hand-painted green leaves in swags with an antique gold rope design that twists around the bucket. Of special interest is the little hand-painted vasculum – decorated with honeysuckles, butterflies, and other insects – used for collecting and carrying botanical samples or seeds.

◆　◆　◆　◆

▶ *OLD enamelware revamped.*

HALF-LIDDED WATERING CAN

This sweet little Edwardian watering can, painted in a rich dark green, is decorated with a single spray of pink roses. The handle has hand-painted gold leaves on it, and the outer rims and handle are highlighted in gold. The cutting for this project has to be absolutely meticulous. The paper is hand-painted and, once the work is under several layers of varnish, it really does appear to be painted on the can.

• materials list •

HALF-LIDDED WATERING CAN or similar piece
PREPARATION
Small can of red oxide metal primer
An old 1 inch (2.5cm) brush
Mineral spirits
PAINTING
Small can of very dark green flat or semigloss
  latex paint
1 inch (2.5cm) brush, or smaller
DÉCOUPAGE
Good-quality, hand-painted wrapping paper
  with sprays of roses
Small sharp scissors
Craft knife
Wallpaper paste
Glue brush
Pasting board
Small sponge or paper towels
ANTIQUE GOLD
Small tubes of gold and raw umber artists'
  acrylics
No. 4 artist's brush
Lidded container or jar
Water to mix
VARNISHING
Tack cloth
Small can of satin polyurethane varnish or
  shellac
1 inch (2.5cm) brush

• preparation •

1 Prepare the can as described on pages 15–18.
2 When the red oxide is completely dry, apply three coats of dark green latex paint to ensure good dense coverage. By turning the can upside down to apply the second coat, no small part of the surface will be left unpainted. Prop the lid open a little to avoid sticking, and leave paint to dry between coats. Push the end of the brush into the spout and make sure that the inside of the handle is painted. When you are satisfied with the surface, leave to dry.

• découpage •

1 Select blooms for their color and shape to decorate the sides and the top of the can. Cut out each spray with great care: first cut the fine inside stems by making an initial incision with the scissor points; this gives you plenty of paper to hold. Cut the outer stems, and so forth, last. Try not to remove any of the thorns because they look wonderful against the dark background, and remember to serrate the edges of the leaves.

If you have difficulty with long curling stems, cut them into sections and butt them together when you stick them onto the surface of the can; the seam will not be noticeable.
2 Turn each cutout face down onto the pasting board and apply the glue evenly, brushing it out over the edges to make sure they are covered. Use a craft knife to lift delicate curling stems from the board and for positioning on the can. Work out any air bubbles and excess glue with your fingers and wipe it off carefully with damp paper towels. When the surface is flat, press down the edges. Rinse fingers frequently because the glue will remove the surface from the paper.
3 When the design is complete, let it dry. Using a damp sponge or paper towel, remove the glue from the background and surface of the work, being careful not to scuff the edges. Leave to dry.

• finishing •

Apply an antique gold finish to the rim and small handle, as described on page 13. Using the same paint, decorate the large handle with leaves as described on page 22. Leave to dry, then varnish as described on pages 13–14.

▶ *THE SIMPLICITY of this decoration is most effective.*

"PRETTY AS A PITCHER"

Lovely old Victorian and Edwardian swan-neck pitchers, in their time known also as ewers, are becoming difficult to find. This is a pity, because they are highly decorative and most useful. They can sometimes be found at garage sales, rummage sales, and in antiques stores – ask a dealer to look out for one. Pitchers have great decorative potential, and look delightful painted in black, traditional dark green, or paint-finished in parchment or pastel colors.

• materials list •

SWAN-NECK PITCHER
PREPARATION
Small can of red oxide metal primer
1 inch (2.5cm) brush
Mineral spirits
Paper towels
PAINTING
Small can of flat or semigloss latex paint in the
 color of your choice
1 inch (2.5cm) brush
DÉCOUPAGE
Floral wrapping paper
Small sharp scissors
Craft knife
Wallpaper paste
Glue brush • Pasting board
Small sponge or paper towels
ANTIQUE GOLD
Tubes of gold and raw umber artists' acrylics
No. 4 or 5 artist's brush
Lidded container or jar
Water to mix
VARNISHING
Tack cloth
Small can of satin polyurethane varnish or
 shellac
1 inch (2.5cm) brush
Mineral spirits

• preparation •

1 Prepare the jug as instructed on pages 15–18.
2 With your hand inside it, apply the first coat of paint to the inside of the handle and the outer surface. Stand the jug upside down and paint the base. Leave to dry. Hold by the handle for the second coat, and paint inside as far as the neck seam. Leave to dry. Three coats will be necessary to ensure adequate coverage.
3 If you have used a cream topcoat, you may wish to apply a parchment paint-finish at this stage (see page 20).

• découpage •

1 Cut out a good selection of flowers and leaves.
2 Turn each cutout face down onto the pasting board and brush on the glue evenly, making sure that the edges are covered. Lift with a craft knife and position on the jug. Press gently, working out excess glue and air bubbles with your fingers until the paper is flat. Press down the edges and wipe away excess glue with damp paper towels.
3 When the decoration is finished and the glue has dried, clean up the surface of the paper and background with damp paper towels. Leave to dry.

• finishing •

Apply an antique gold finish to the rims of the jug, as described on page 13, and leave to dry. Then varnish as instructed on pages 13–14, being careful to avoid dribbles from the base of the handle and around the top rim. All the jugs in the photographs have at least 10 coats of varnish.

▶ *IVY AND OLD roses look lovely on either background.*

SOPHISTICATED TALL black
Victorian and Edwardian
swan-necked pitchers, which
have been elaborately
decorated and gilded, stand
beside an early nineteenth-
century tin hatbox,
hand-painted with wild roses
by the author.

◆

FLORAL PLANTERS

In this section you will find three planters, initially similar (though of varying size) but all quite different now that they are decorated. The largest is painted in black with a simple decoration of nasturtiums, very vibrant and sophisticated, photographed with red cyclamen.

BRILLIANT RED cyclamen complement this design beautifully.

◆

◆ *materials list* ◆

METAL PLANTER
PREPARATION
Small can of red oxide primer
An old 1 inch (2.5cm) brush
Mineral spirits
Paper towels
PAINTING
Small can of black flat or semigloss latex
   paint
1 inch (2.5cm) brush
DÉCOUPAGE
Wrapping paper with nasturtium motif
Small sharp scissors
Craft knife
Wallpaper adhesive
Glue brush
Pasting board
Small sponge or paper towels
Piece of white chalk
ANTIQUE GOLD
Tubes of gold and raw umber artists'
   acrylics
No. 5 artist's brush
Lidded container or jar
Water to mix
VARNISHING
Tack cloth
Small can of satin polyurethane varnish or
   shellac
1 inch (2.5cm) brush
FINAL TOUCHES
Small amount of self-adhesive baize or felt
   for base
Kitchen scissors

◆ *preparation* ◆

1 Prepare the planter as described on pages 15–18.
2 When the red oxide is dry, apply at least three coats of black latex paint to all surfaces of the planter, allowing the paint to dry between coats.

◆ *découpage* ◆

1 Cut the nasturtiums and their curling stems meticulously, because the color contrast against the black will be a knock-out and untidy cutting very obvious. If you find the stems difficult, cut them into sections and butt them together when you stick them to the surface; it will not be noticeable. You may find it helpful to turn the planter on its side and lay the design on it to get an idea of how it will look. Draw around the flowers and stems with chalk, marking out their shape: this will be a good guide when you place the delicate pasted stems into position.
2 Turn each cutout face down onto the pasting board and brush on the glue evenly all over the surface. Lift from the board with a craft knife, turn right side up (do not panic when it curls up), and stick to the planter by pressing very gently with a rolling movement of the fingers, working out the excess glue which can be removed with paper towels. When the air bubbles are pressed out and the surface is flat, press down the edges. (*NOTE* When working with fine stems, it is important to keep fingers clean, otherwise the surface of the paper will stick to them and be ruined.)
3 When the decoration is complete, leave it to dry. Clean up the work, removing dried glue from the background and decoration with a damp sponge or paper towel. Leave to dry.

◆ *finishing* ◆

Apply an antique gold finish to the top rim, as described on page 13, ensuring a neat finish on the inside, too. Leave to dry, then varnish as described on pages 13–14. The inside of the planter will require about two coats.

◆ *final touches* ◆

Cut a piece of self-adhesive felt or baize to shape and stick to the bottom of the planter to protect furniture, and give a professional finish.

 HERE IS THE BLACK PLANTER AGAIN, *this time photographed in a huge Victorian conservatory*
with the harvest of summer gathered in and piled around it. The nasturtiums are actually
growing up through the garden table!

ROSE PLANTER

ROSES DECORATE *a soft ocher paint-finished background on a medium-sized planter, which has a soft brown paint on the inside to add a little contrast. Follow all the guidelines for the previous planter, varying the color of the topcoat of paint. A three-color sponge finish has been applied in yellow ocher, Chinese white, and cadmium yellow artists' acrylics using the technique described on pages 19–20.*

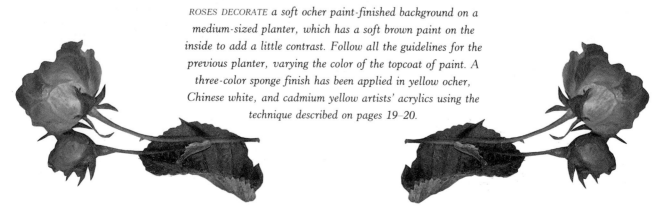

◆

ROSEBUD PLANTER

FADED OLD ROSEBUDS *on twisted ribbons are a simple and*
pretty adornment for the smallest planter. This one is painted
in dark umbery-green outside and a strong cayenne inside.

◆

◆

RIBBONS AND ROSES PLANTER

SWAGS, RIBBONS, AND ROSES *adorn this planter, which is an old enamel washing bowl rejuvenated with spring-green paint on the outside, and cream inside sponged directly from the can with the same green.*

◆

13
UNUSUAL ANTIQUES

Throughout this final chapter you will find several of my favorite objects with which I am now unable to part.

I hope that they will both inspire you and demonstrate to you the incredible diversity of objects there are to decorate, and the many interesting possibilities and ideas which present themselves afresh with each new project.

Three of these (the hatbox, the nutmeg box, and the ham boiler) are decorated with identical paper, although not the same flowers, and the background colors crop up more than once. The overall theme is "swags, ribbons, and roses." I do hope you will enjoy looking through them, and that you will be fired with enthusiasm to collect a few unusual (and cheap) antiques. Happy hunting.

♦ ♦ ♦ ♦

▶ *HATBOX This charming nineteenth-century tin hatbox in perfect condition has been given the "swags, ribbons, and roses" treatment. A dear friend of mine, Marianne Grace, decorated it using the same paper as the enamel bowl planter on page 133, choosing the open blooms and spacing them out individually into deep swags. The roses on the lid have a hand-painted twisted ribbon running through them.*

Old hatboxes can still be found in antiques and secondhand stores specializing in tinware, although rarely in this pristine condition. Have you looked in your attic lately?

*The hatbox was prepared as described on pages 15–18, painted in a dark umbery-green semigloss latex paint and gilded **after** varnishing with liquid gold.*

♦

DOMED TRUNK

DOMED TRUNK *Isn't this darling? – a little Victorian trunk in such a lovely shape. Unusually, it still has its padlock. I felt that it should be a very feminine piece, so I painted it in this delightful soft turquoise and decorated it with violas cut from a paper which depicts French textiles. I am thrilled with the result, especially as I have never come across another like it.*

NUTMEG BOX

NUTMEG BOX *The tin box is divided into sections inside with a circular grater in the center. Prepared as usual for tinware (pages 15–18), and decorated with poppies and roses on a deep sea-green background with hand-painted gold leaves. Very simple to do and a stunning little object.*

HAM BOILER

HAM BOILER *Rounder than a fish steamer, the old ham boiler has a lovely oval shape with a domed lid. The moment I spotted it I visualized it decorated in a regency style. You may recognize both the paper and background paint from earlier projects. I think the gorgeous turquoise and delicate roses look perfect.*

I adore this giftwrap paper, which depicts nineteenth-century French floral textiles; all very different, but ideal for découpage. The paper is extremely thin and requires careful cutting and pasting, but, as you see, the end result is well worth the trouble.

MAIL TRAY

MAIL PRESENTATION TRAY *This metal tray was prepared as usual for tinware (see pages 15–18), then painted dark country-green with a simple design of rose stems. Since the handle is brass, the plate was left ungilded.*

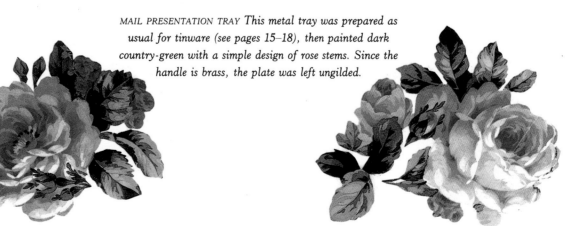

VICTORIAN FOOTWARMER

VICTORIAN FOOTWARMER *This is the sweetest thing and would originally have been in plain metal, filled with hot water, and slipped under the cushion of a Victorian footstool. It was prepared as usual for tinware (see pages 15–18), and painted in black semigloss latex paint before applying the découpage decoration of water lilies, complete with kingfisher. The leaves are hand-painted in antique gold acrylics.*

ACKNOWLEDGEMENTS

Thanks to the following for making this book possible: Virginia Hiller for suggesting I write a book in the first place, and for introducing me to Di Lewis. Di Lewis for her wonderfully inspired photography throughout the book; it has been both a privilege and a pleasure to work with her, and I have gained much from her experienced eye and professional guidance; she has inspired and encouraged me with her ideas, enthusiasm, and drive, and I value her continued friendship. Polly Mobsby of Smart Arts for her kindness and patience in allowing us to photograph in her lovely home and grounds on countless occasions, and for supplying textiles, antiques, and props. Marianne Grace, a fine artist, gardener, and dear friend, for her beautiful artwork in the book, her calm countenance and sense of humor, and her inspirational ideas, many of them incorporated in this book. Vivienne Wells and Brenda Morrison at David & Charles for their trust in a novice author, allowing me to get on with the book without pressure; for their encouragement and support throughout. Marianne and Peter Methley for allowing us to photograph in their beautiful home, and Lizzie and Simon Smith for letting us photograph their gorgeous children, Annabel and Charlie, for the nursery project. Terry "Whoosh" Penny of Smart Arts for making all the screens in the book and the unusually shaped headboard in the shortest possible time. Caspari Ltd., National Gallery Publications Ltd., and Jemima Haddock of Alan Hutchison Limited, all of whom generously supplied their wonderful papers. Sandra Wall-Armitage, a skillful botanical artist and teacher, whose deep love of flowers shows in her work. Her beautiful papers are used often throughout the book and were certainly a challenge and a true test of cutting! (I have tried hard to find the owners of all the papers used. Where this has not been possible, please accept my apologies.) Laura Ashley Ltd. for supplying their lovely rich red "Aragon" fabric for the photographs on page 90. Ken Haskell, head gardener extraordinaire, for his fabulous roses on page 75, and Nina Lockyer for the variegated leaves and flowers from her garden. Finally, many thanks and love to my family and friends for their constant help and support.

◆

GUIDE TO SUPPLIERS

• *papers* •

Harry N. Abrams Inc.
100 Fifth Avenue
New York
NY 10011 USA
Telephone (212) 206-7715

Adventures in Crafts
P.O. Box 6058
Yorkville Station
New York
NY 10128 USA
Telephone (212) 410-9793

Artifacts
P.O. Box 3399
Palestine
TX 75802 USA
Telephone (903) 729-4178

Artist and Display Supply
9015 West Burleigh Street
Milwaukee
WI 53222 USA
Telephone (414) 442-9100

Dover Publications
31 East 2nd Street
Mineola
NY 11501 USA
Telephone (516) 294-7000
Telephone in Canada (416) 445-3333

Flax Artist Materials
P.O. Box 7216
San Francisco
CA 94120-7216 USA
Telephone (415) 468-7530

Kate's Paperie
561 Broadway
New York
NY 11012 USA
Telephone (800) 809-9880

Laila's
1136 Lorimar Drive
Mississauga
Ontario L5S 1R7
Canada
Telephone (905) 795-8955

• *tools and other materials* •

Artist Emporium
106–1135 64th Avenue SE
Calgary
Alberta T2H 2J7
Canada
Telephone (800) 661-8341
        (403) 255-2090

Constantine's
2050 Eastchester Road
Bronx
NY 10461 USA
Telephone (800) 223-8087

Omer DeSerres
334 Ste-Catherine East
Montreal
Quebec H2X 1L7
Canada
Telephone (800) 363-0318
        (514) 842-6637

A.I. Friedman
44 West 18th Street
New York
NY 10011 USA
Telephone (212) 337-8600

Lee Valley
1080 Morrison Drive
Ottawa
Ontario K2H 8K7
Canada
Telephone (800) 267-8767
        (613) 596-0350

Maiwa Handprints
6–1666 Johnston Street
Granville Island, Vancouver
British Columbia V6H 3S2
Canada
Telephone (604) 669-3939

Pearl Paint
308 Canal Street
New York
NY 10013 USA
Telephone (800) 221-6845
(212-431-7932 in NYC and LI)

Sax Arts and Crafts
2405 Calhoun Road
P.O. Box 51710
New Berlin
WI 53151 USA
Telephone (414) 784-6880

Sam Flax, Inc.
425 Park Avenue
New York
NY 10022 USA
Telephone (212) 620-3060

Daniel Smith
4150 First Avenue
Seattle
WA 98134 USA
Telephone (206) 223-9599

D.L. Stevenson & Son
1420 Warden Avenue
Scarborough
Ontario M1R 5A3
Canada
Telephone (416) 755-7795

Garrett Wade
161 Avenue of Americas
New York
NY 10013 USA
Telephone (212) 807-1155

INDEX